THE
CATALAN
KITCHEN

FROM MOUNTAINS TO CITY AND SEA – RECIPES FROM SPAIN'S CULINARY HEART

EMMA WARREN

Smith
Street
Books

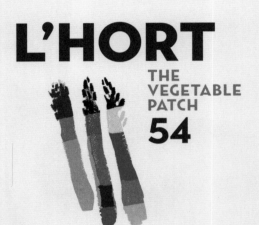

LA COSTA

THE COAST

84

EL CAMP

THE COUNTRYSIDE

120

SALSES I BROUS

BROTHS & SAUCES

230

INTRODUCTION

'Benvinguts' (welcome) to *The Catalan Kitchen*, where seasonal produce, innovative cooking and a passionate dedication towards food, cultivation and heritage come together to celebrate a unique cuisine that's intrinsically bound to history, creativity and identity. Like its people, Catalan food is fiercely independent, with a culinary history all of its own.

Catalunya is a welcoming place. Life there is generous, familiar, open and sharing, and you can take it into your heart and feel you've discovered it all on your own. It's a personal affair, which can be as intimate and sophisticated as you like, and the love in return is always unconditional and everlasting. This all-embracing approach to life is extended to the Catalan attitude towards food and, as a result, much of the province's produce and local dishes are respected, nurtured and revered.

It can be argued that Catalan gastronomy is more Mediterranean than Spanish and this, in part, can be attributed to the invasion and resulting occupation of numerous cultures over the centuries. Throughout history, Greeks, Moors, Phoenicians and Romans all left their mark on the Iberian Peninsula, whether in olive oil, bread or the 'cazuela', a clay cooking vessel that's still used today. The Arabs introduced new agricultural and farming practices, such as irrigation channels for cultivating olives, nuts and rice, while the Jews brought eggplants (aubergines), artichokes and spices to the diet. Closer to home, in addition to the spoils of war, the Crown of Aragon brought back ingredients from Sicily, Sardinia and Naples, where locals turned them into dishes, such as Canelons (page 158) and Rossejat (page 112), which are still regularly eaten today.

On the flipside, starting in the Middle Ages and into the Renaissance, Catalan cuisine was one of the very first to expand beyond its geographical boundaries and become sought-after throughout Europe. Catalunya's position in the Mediterranean made it a wealthy trading hub, where merchants would come and go, taking back to their homes the ingredients and dishes they learned to love. In addition, Catalunya's neighbours, Andorra and the regions of southern France – Provence, the Pyrenees and Roussillon – have blurred their borders through traditional recipes, be they savoury or sweet, coastal or inland. Over time, variations in technique may have changed, but the end results signify the dual influences these regions have always mutually possessed.

Today, Catalunya, like any other major European province, is a cosmopolitan and mulitcultural society, which experiences the same socio-economic benefits and problems that any modern, democratic country provides. Over the years, people from Morocco, Argentina, China and Africa have all migrated to this part of Europe, and there has been a large influx of Andulcians to Catalunya, all contributing to the taste, flavour and culture that make up modern Catalan life.

The ability of the Catalan people to embrace these cultures and harmonise, adapt and unify is proudly protected. Catalunya is a nurturing place, safe but edgy, confident but not intimidating. It's overwhelmingly captivating and full of charisma, appeal, character and personality. It adopts you and protects you and you trust that it will provide and not disappoint. These distinct characteristics are inevitably extended to Catalan food and cooking.

The Catalan kitchen is eclectic; it can give you sophistication in one dish and, in the next, surprise you with a rustic simplicity that is both traditional and flavoursome. It is this combined attitude, which makes it one of the richest and broadest cuisines, not only in Spain, but throughout the Mediterranean.

Catalan cuisine can be described as many things. Some say that it is avant garde, mysterious and charming. Perhaps this is a reflection of the fact that the province holds more Michelin stars than any other region in Spain, and that it is always drawing on the history of its influences to push the boundaries, innovate and invent with fondness, affection and respect. Novelties aside, Catalan cooking is inherently linked to tradition and the past, yet it also leans into the future, but with a familiarity so that even the most abstract of dishes tie back to something already understood.

I learnt to cook professionally in Catalunya and on the Balearic Island of Mallorca. I learnt the languages there, both Spanish and Catalan. I lived alone, and worked and travelled around its vast and diverse landscape. I fell in love, made everlasting friendships and matured from a young backpacker into a woman of the world. In writing this book, I wanted to share the spirit and intrinsic nature of the Catalan kitchen. To cook Catalan food is to immerse yourself in the seasons, to understand the importance of local produce and how food connects us all. It reminds us how to share, be a part of a community and to learn and practise the very art of living.

The Catalan Kitchen is a collection of authentic dishes that are regularly eaten throughout the province. Some of them are new, while some are more traditional, but all of them are well-loved by the locals who make them. Our journey begins with 'Pica Pica' (to pick), which features a selection of small dishes (one might be tempted to say 'tapas', but this isn't strictly Catalan) often found in bars and restaurants, at cocktail parties and in homes, where Sunday lunch and family gatherings always commence with a few plates to share while waiting for the main meal.

'L'Hort' (the vegetable patch) is a true celebration of the seasons and here you will find simple side dishes and salads to accompany your favourite protein. Take a trip to your local market, fall in love with the seasonal produce on offer and take it home to create something spectacular.

You don't have to spend long in Catalunya to understand the importance of seafood in the Catalan diet. Anchovies, sardines, bacallà (salt cod) and shellfish feature heavily, either celebrated in their own right or paired with meat in 'mar i muntanya' (sea and mountain) dishes, which epitomise Catalan cuisine. It is in 'La Costa' (the coast) that you will also find the classic paella and Catalunya's own distinctive take on this much-loved recipe, the Rossejat.

'El Camp' (the countryside) is all about warmth and comfort with stews, braises, roasts and grills from the mountains and hillsides. It also celebrates Catalan charcuterie, which is considered some of the best in the world, due to Catalunya's unique climate and traditional farming techniques. As Spain's largest supplier of pigs, pork makes a regular appearance in Catalan dishes in all its myriad forms, from smallgoods and sausages, such as the famous chorizo, to pâtés and terrines.

'Barna Moderna' (modern Barcelona) offers a little of what you can find today in the bustling streets, plazas and laneways of Catalunya's capital city. Drawing from the catalogue of the past, and twisted, tweaked and transformed into something new, here you will find a modern approach to familiar dishes.

'Dolços' (desserts) are very popular in Catalunya, and festivals throughout the year are marked by the making and eating of traditional cakes and sweets. Steeped in tradition and history, these recipes can be found in every Catalan home. Of course, you don't need a festival to indulge in dessert, and this chapter also celebrates the everyday sweets available on 'menús del dia' (menus of the day) throughout the province.

Finally, 'Salses i Brous' (sauces and broths) brings together perhaps the most important recipes of the Catalan cooking repertoire. They are the glue that binds ingredients together, completing and complementing dishes to give them that distinct flavour, which truly sets the Catalan cuisine apart from the rest of the world.

KITCHEN NOTES

At the time of writing this book, the Catalan government has been politically and democratically campaigning for independence from Spain. Out of respect for this I have used the local name 'Catalunya' throughout the book, which refers to the autonomous community in Spain. In the recipes, I have only used the Spanish word for an ingredient, name or dish where the English-speaking reader would more likely identify with that word than the English translation; for example, paella and tortilla (instead of Spanish omelette).

OILS, VINEGARS & PIMENTÓNS

When a recipe calls for extra virgin olive oil, select a good-quality, semi-mild oil with a fruity flavour. Always use cold-pressed oil and try to buy as local as possible, to ensure freshness. Below are a few varieties of extra virgin olive oil regularly used in Catalan cuisine.

ARBEQUINA refers to the type of olive grown in Alt Urgell in Lleida, an area awarded DOP (Protected Designation of Origin) status. Here, the climate, land and local farming practices ensure a high-quality, fruity, dense and fragrant extra virgin olive oil that's mainly produced by local co-ops. The greener the oil, the younger the fruit, and the spicier and more bitter the resulting product.

SUAVE is a light extra virgin olive oil that's mild in flavour and taste. Made using more mature olives, it's fantastic for frying eggs, using in cakes or making condiments, such as Allioli (page 244) and Maionesa (page 245).

TRUFFLE OIL – Catalans often infuse truffle offcuts with a light-tasting olive oil. If you'd like to make your own, add a small sliver to a bottle of extra virgin olive oil and infuse for a minimum of six days in a warm place.

JAMÓN OIL is made with the ends of the jamón that you can't quite get through the automatic slicer without cutting a finger off! To make your own, infuse 100 g (3½ oz) jamón slices in 185 ml (6 fl oz/¾ cup) of extra virgin olive oil for a minimum of four days in a 20–30°C (70–85°F) spot.

LEMON OIL is perfect for adding to salad dressings and drizzling over fish. Combine the peel, removing all the pith, of ½ lemon with 185 ml (6 fl oz/¾ cup) light-tasting olive oil and set aside for a minimum of four days at 20–30°C (70–85°F).

SHERRY VINEGAR – Although not recognised by DOP in Catalunya, this ingredient is regularly used in all facets of Catalan cooking. The base is actually fermented sherry wine, which is aged for a minimum of six months.

AGED BALSAMIC VINEGAR is often used to dress salads. Balsamic reduction is also popular in Catalunya, where it's used to decorate dishes at the end of cooking.

WHITE AND RED WINE VINEGARS are used for pickling produce or blended with sherry vinegar to lighten the taste of a dish, where sherry vinegar alone would otherwise be too strong.

PIMENTÓN is known as paprika in the western world but true paprika is Hungarian, which uses different varieties of red capsicums (bell peppers) for drying and grinding. Pimentón 'dulce' refers to sweet pimentón, pimentón 'picante' is spicy, while pimentón 'ahumado' means smoked.

50% Dry Sherry. 17/2
25% Red Wine Vin. 2018
25% W. Wine Vin.

PICA
PICA
TO PICK

The Catalans don't really 'do tapas', instead they 'pica pica!'.

This ingrained custom of sharing an array of small, bite-sized portions of food – a little bit of this and a little bit of that – is usually enjoyed at the beginning of a long dining session. 'Pica pica' are presented together at the table for guests to help themselves, an informal experience to whet the appetite and an opportunity for friends and family to catch up and share news before the main meal.

This first chapter features classic and much-loved Catalan 'pica pica' recipes, along with a few larger dishes or 'raciónes', which can be served as snacks, canapès, tapas, aperetifs, pintxos, hors d'oeuvres, finger food, entrées or small bites to pick at and enjoy at the start of a meal, whether it's family Sunday lunch or a more fancy degustation menu.

You can, of course, also simply sit down to a big feast of 'pica pica' and be more than satisfied, and you'll often find Catalans in their 'second lounge room' at the local bar tucking in to a large variety of plates, while watching their favourite football team play the weekly match.

Going out for 'pica pica' is a favourite pastime for most Catalans. From the bustling centre of Barcelona to rural town squares, locals and tourists alike will hop from place to place, often along the same route, enjoying each bar's specialty dish 'de la casa' (house special) before moving on to the next. Often simple in their presentation, plates might consist of warm local olives, white anchovies, croquettes, chargrilled vegetables, or a salad made with produce from the surrounding region or even a neighbour's backyard.

Be sure to leave room, though. As delicious as 'pica pica' are, Catalans will nearly always follow up with a main meal and, of course, dessert! So, take your time, set aside several hours to eat, and enjoy the variety and diversity of the true Catalan dining experience.

AMETTLES MARCONAS

MARCONA ALMONDS

Out of the more than 100 types of almonds grown in Spain, the Marcona, 'Queen of Almonds' is a native botanical variety characterised by its round, flat shape and soft texture. Inside its hard, non-porous exterior lies a high level of concentrated oils, making it a rich, intensely flavoured, sweet and juicy nut. Produced in the Tarragona region of Catalunya, it is the most expensive, sought-after almond for making 'turrón' (Spanish nougat), marzipan and other traditional cakes and pastries. Outside of Spain, Marcona often refers to the skinless, toasted, salted snack widely marketed throughout the rest of Europe and the US, even though the almonds used may not be their original varietal namesake.

This recipe is traditionally served as an aperitif or snack, chopped and sprinkled over salads or braised meats, in salted caramel toffees and stuffed dates or in old-school devils on horsebacks.

Makes about 300 g (10½ oz)

300 g (10½ oz) blanched almonds
1½ tablespoons extra virgin
   olive oil
1 sprig rosemary
1 garlic clove, smashed
2 teaspoons butter
1 teaspoon salt flakes

Place the almonds in a large bowl, cover with lukewarm water and allow to stand for 1 hour. This will rehydrate any old, dry almonds there might be and enable them to absorb more flavours in the pan.

Drain and spread the almonds in an even, single layer on a clean tea towel or paper towel to air-dry for about 20 minutes. Alternatively, put the almonds in a very low 60°C (140°F) fan-fored oven for 6 minutes to dry out.

Heat the oil, rosemary and garlic in a large saucepan or frying pan over medium–high heat. Toss through the almonds and stir to toast evenly. Once the almonds start to take on some colour and turn golden, add the butter to the pan and swirl to coat. Continue sautéing for 2 minutes.

Remove from the heat, stir through the salt flakes and transfer to paper towel to briefly drain.

Serve immediately while still warm.

SEITÓNS

WHITE ANCHOVIES

El seitó (boquerón in Spanish) is the small fresh fish used to make salted anchovies (anxova salaó). They are also preserved in vinegar and eaten as the ultimate aperitif during late Sunday morning vermouth (vermùt) sessions in the neighbourhood (barri) with mates, debriefing about the 'discoteca' the night before.

A lot of bars will serve 'seitóns' with a small plate of homemade 'patata' crisps doused in spicy sauce and some stuffed olives on the house to wash down your 'vermùt' or 'cañita' (small beer) with, to get you back on track before everyone disperses to their parents' house for Sunday family lunch. It's also one of the only times you'll see Catalans turning things a bit spicy with the fiery local salsa 'espinaler', similar to Tabasco.

Catalunya has access to great-quality fish conserves and some of the best anchovies in the world come from L'Escala, Girona.

Serves 4

150–200 g (5–7 oz) white anchovies in vinegar

2½ tablespoons extra virgin olive oil

1 teaspoon sweet pimentón

1 dried ñora pepper, rehydrated in hot water, seeds removed and sliced into strips (see note on page 236)

160 g (5½ oz) bag good-quality salted potato chips (crisps)

Tabasco or Mexican hot sauce, to drizzle

green olives, stuffed with pimientos, to serve

Pat the anchovies dry with paper towel. Transfer to a glass or ceramic dish and drizzle with the oil. Sprinkle over the pimentón and dried pepper strips.

Tip the potato chips into a bowl and drizzle with the hot sauce.

Serve the anchovies and chips with the stuffed olives and a glass of red vermouth with loads of ice and a wedge of orange.

PA AMB TOMÀQUET

BREAD WITH TOMATO

This sacred national dish is a major part of the Catalan identity and relies completely on the quality of all five ingredients. It is the simplest yet most fussed-over dish in Catalan cuisine. Served with almost every meal, many a heated discussion can lead to stern disagreements after debating intricacies, such as the best tomatoes or oil to use, or which order you must follow to create the most perfect result.

As with most longstanding traditional Mediterranean cuisines and dishes, the stayers are usually those born from a need to limit waste and deal with excess. Like gazpacho, 'pa amb tomàquet' is a way to use up excess bread, rehydrated and back on the table to fill and nourish the family.

But tomatoes all year round? Yes, the 'tomàquet de penjar' or 'ramellet' is a hung-together cluster of vine tomatoes known as winter tomatoes, which are available throughout the year in Catalunya. Grown with low-volume irrigation, they have lost most of their acidity and make for an intensely flavoursome and fleshy fruit.

Serves 4

4 slices rustic sourdough white bread
1 garlic clove, peeled
2 very ripe medium tomatoes, halved
1 tablespoon extra virgin olive oil
1 teaspoon salt flakes

Toast, grill or barbecue the bread slowly to dry it out and harden it slightly. Gently rub the garlic clove over each slice – the abrasiveness of the toasted bread will cut the garlic across its surface.

Firmly squash the tomato onto the bread, cut side down, and squeeze as you rub to release the juice and flesh.

Drizzle with olive oil, sprinkle evenly with salt and bon profiti!

ARBEQUINAS CASOLANES

WILD OLIVES

The Arbequina is one of the most juicy, buttery, peppery and oil-rich varieties of olive. Its flesh is ideal for oil production due to its high fat content, serving as the most essential base of all Catalan cuisine. Grown mainly in and around the volcanic mineral-rich area of Les Garrigues, Lleida, it originally takes its name from the small village of 'Arbeca', where there are 1000-year-old trees still in harvest.

Its small but meaty and nutty flesh makes for a great table olive, too. You will often find it served in its own oil, with a mix of wild herbs picked from the surrounding hills where they thrive.

Makes about 500 g (1 lb 2 oz)

400 g (14 oz) brined Arbequina olives, wild olives or good-quality mixed olives
peel of ½ orange, pith removed
2 sprigs thyme
2 fresh bay leaves
2 sprigs marjoram or oregano
1 teaspoon aniseed or 1 star anise
1 teaspoon fennel seeds
2 garlic cloves, quartered
2 fennel fronds (optional)
80 ml (2½ fl oz/⅓ cup) extra virgin olive oil
crusty bread, to serve

Drain the olives from their brine and place in a large bowl. Cut the orange peel into strips and place in the bowl, along with the remaining ingredients except the olive oil.

Warm the oil in a large saucepan or frying pan over low heat. Add the olive mixture and gently warm through, stirring continuously, for 8–10 minutes, until the flavours have infused.

Transfer to a serving bowl and serve warm with ripped crusty bread to mop up the flavour-filled oil.

ESQUEIXADA I EMPEDRAT

TWO SALT COD SALADS

These two salads, both containing bacallà (salt cod), are very close cousins and are regularly seen on menus throughout Catalunya. Esqueixada – meaning to tear, shred or rip – is centred around the bacallà. Empedrat – meaning cobblestones because of the way the salad mimics little pebbles – comes from L'Empordà in the province of Girona. It shares similar ingredients with the esqueixada, but instead includes white beans and the bacallà simply as a garnish.

Serves 4 per recipe

Esqueixada

500 g (1 lb 2 oz) bacallà (salt cod) fillets or fresh blue eye, haddock or rock ling fillets

1 kg (2 lb 3 oz) rock salt (if using fresh fish fillets)

2 medium vine-ripened tomatoes, cut into wedges

½ white onion, thinly sliced

½ red capsicum (bell pepper), finely diced

½ green capsicum (bell pepper), finely diced

8 whole black olives

80 ml (2½ fl oz/⅓ cup) extra virgin olive oil

30 ml (1 fl oz) sherry vinegar

Empedrat

250 g (9 oz) bacallà (salt cod) fillets or fresh blue eye, haddock or rock ling fillets

500 g (1 lb 2 oz) rock salt (if using fresh fish fillets)

2 medium vine-ripened tomatoes, cut into wedges

400 g (14 oz) tin haricot (navy) beans, rinsed and drained

½ white onion, finely diced

½ red capsicum (bell pepper), finely diced

½ green capsicum (bell pepper), finely diced

80 ml (2½ fl oz/⅓ cup) extra virgin olive oil

30 ml (1 fl oz) sherry vinegar

small handful parsley, chopped

If using purchased bacallà, submerge the fish in cold water for 8–12 hours (depending on the thickness of the fish), changing the water every 4 hours. Tear the flesh away from any skin, bones and wings and taste for texture and saltiness. It should be soft with a hint of salt. If the bacallà is still too salty or dry, return it to fresh, clean water and change the water regularly until you've reached the desired texture and flavour.

If you want to make your own bacallà, spread half the rock salt on a baking tray and place the fresh fish on top. Cover with the remaining salt and bake in a preheated 180°C (350°F) fan-forced oven for 15 minutes. Allow to cool, then remove the encrusted salt and rinse the fish under cold running water until all the salt is removed. Flake the flesh roughly into pieces and rinse again if the flavour is still too salty for your liking.

Place the bacallà and the remaining salad ingredients in large serving bowls, mix well and set aside for 10 minutes to allow the flavours to infuse.

Serve with Pa amb tomàquet (see page 22).

Empedrat

Esqueixada

XATÓ

CHATEAU SALAD

'Xató', from the word Chateau – refers to the size and decadence of this salad, which showcases the best produce from the Catalan region. So famous is it that it has its own festival called 'La ruta del Xató' southeast of Barcleona, starting in the Garraf region, then inland over to the wine region of El Penedès and down into the north of the Costa Daurada. Each town has its own variation of the salsa romesco and each claims the origin of this much-loved salad, traditionally eaten in Lent during the winter months.

The thick dip consistency of the salsa is hearty and wholesome and, paired with the bitterness of the greens, it never gets tired. It's Cataluyna's version of hummus and crudités in a salad, but showcasing the sea.

For a traditional Catalan fisherman's lunch, serve this dish with some Pa amb tomàquet (see page 22) on the side.

Serves 4

- 150 g (5½ oz) bacallà (salt cod) fillets
- 1 frisée (curly endive), washed, dark green leaves discarded
- 150 g (5½ oz) tuna chunks in olive oil
- 4 salted anchovy fillets
- 2 tablespoons Arbequinas or green manzanilla olives
- 280 g (10 oz/1 cup) Salsa romesco (see page 236)

Submerge the bacallà in cold water for 4–8 hours (depending on the thickness of the fish), changing the water every 2 hours. Tear the flesh away from any skin, bones and wings and taste for texture and saltiness. It should be soft with a hint of salt. If the bacallà is still too salty or dry, return it to fresh, clean water and change the water regularly until you've reached the desired texture and flavour.

Roughly pull any large frisée leaves apart, remove any excess water with a clean tea towel and place the leaves on a large serving platter. Place the bacallà, tuna, anchovies and olives on top of the frisée and finish with dollops of salsa romesco.

ESCALIVADA

ASH-ROASTED VEGETABLES

Traditionally, this dish is barbecued over coals. 'Escalivar' means to cook in ashes or directly on hot embers, a technique also used for cooking Catalunya's famous 'patates al caliu' (jacket potatoes). In the past, Catalans didn't have access to an abundance of resources, such as gas, and even today a lot of homes still run off refillable gas bottles (butano). You can hear the peddlers banging bottles all day long and yelling 'butanoooooo' around the streets.

An oven can be used for this recipe, but it will sacrifice the taste and spirit of the dish. If you are cooking inside, a gas stovetop is a better option. Put some foil down around your elements before you make a huge mess.

There are many ways to eat this dish: on its own with good-quality tinned sardines or anchovies, as a side for grilled fish or meats, or on top of the famous Coca de recapte (see page 44).

Serves 4–6

2 large brown onions, unpeeled
2 medium eggplants (aubergines)
2 red capsicums (bell peppers)
1 garlic clove, thinly sliced
80 ml (2½ fl oz/⅓ cup) extra virgin olive oil
2 tablespoons Salsa de julivert (see page 240), to drizzle
salt flakes, to serve

Fire up a charcoal or wood-fired barbecue 40–60 minutes before you want to start grilling. You want to get it to a point where the coals have stopped smoking and you can't hold your palm 15 cm (6 in) above the coals for more than 4 seconds without really feeling a sting.

Using long tongs, first place the onions in the embers for 5–6 minutes, as they'll need a bit more time than the other ingredients. Make two or three pricks in the eggplants to prevent them exploding and carefully add to the embers, followed by the red capsicums. Using tongs, turn the vegetables often so they don't completely blacken or overcook on one side.

Meanwhile, combine the garlic and olive oil in a small jar and set aside to infuse.

When the vegetables have just softened and are well-coloured all over, carefully remove them from the embers, shake off as much ash as possible and place in a large stainless steel or heat-retaining bowl. Cover with plastic wrap or foil and let sit to carry on cooking internally for about 20 minutes. You don't want to overcook them on the embers or the flesh will fall apart and lose its sweetness.

Once cool enough to handle, uncover the vegetables and gently peel off all the skins. Do not wash – use a blunt knife or the back of a spoon to remove any unwanted burnt bits. Cut the eggplant and capsicum into strips, separate the onion layers and arrange the vegetables on a serving platter.

Drizzle over the garlic oil and salsa de julivert, sprinkle with salt flakes and enjoy.

AMANIDA
CATALANA

CATALAN SALAD

You can find this combination of salad ingredients in various permutations all over Spain, showcasing what Catalunya has to offer. No matter what the composition, what sets it apart from all the other Spanish table salads is the addition of 'embotits' (charcuterie).

This salad has a bit of everything and ticks most of the major food groups in one big bowl. It is almost always served with all the ingredients presented individually, including the oil, vinegar, salt and pepper, so you can dress the salad as you wish, and to keep the vinegar away from the cured meats.

This version is more akin to a farmers'-style salad you may have found back in the day at an isolated mountain-side pit stop with a wild kitchen garden, but without all the homemade 'embotit' offerings. Sometimes you might get their house chorizo (xoriç), white or black pudding (bull blanc/negre), various types of local sausage, such as 'fuet' or 'llonganissa', cured pork loin (llom de pagés) or a cooked sweet ham option, such as 'pernil dolç', mortadella or jamón.

Serves 4

300 g (10½ oz) iceberg lettuce, roughly torn
2 vine-ripened tomatoes, cut into wedges
8 cooked white asparagus spears (see page 68) or use 300 g (10½ oz) white asparagus from a jar or tin, rinsed and drained
400 g (14 oz) tin hearts of palm (optional), rinsed and drained
1 carrot, shredded on a mandoline
4 radishes, thinly sliced
2 hardboiled eggs, peeled and halved
4 cooked chorizos, thinly sliced
4 slices jamón or prosciutto
4 slices salami
4 slices mortadella, rolled up
8 green olives, stuffed with anchovy

To serve
salt flakes and freshly cracked black pepper
sherry vinegar
good-quality extra virgin olive oil

Arrange all the salad ingredients decoratively in a bowl or on a serving platter in whichever order or design you prefer.

Serve in the centre of the table with the salt and pepper, vinegar and olive oil, so everyone can dress their own salad.

This salad is even better served with Pa amb tomàquet (see page 22).

ENSALADILLA RUSA

RUSSIAN SALAD

This salad, also called the Olivier after the Russian chef who invented it, appears in every Catalan canteen, on school-camp menus, at buffets, tapas bars and in the packaged food section of the supermarket. You can even buy the vegetables pre-cut, par-cooked and frozen, ready to reheat, dress and serve.

Waxy potatoes, such as nicola or kipfler (fingerling) are best for this salad, as they hold together well when cooked. The kipflers also cook quite evenly from the outside in because of their trunk-like shape. It's important to cook the vegetables whole to retain as much flavour as possible and to avoid too much water being absorbed.

Serves 4

1 kg (2 lb 3 oz) kipfler (fingerling) or nicola potatoes, scrubbed clean

2 small carrots or 4 Dutch carrots, scrubbed clean

2 eggs

80 g (2¾ oz/½ cup) fresh or frozen green peas

salt flakes and ground white pepper

1 tablespoon sherry vinegar

1 tablespoon extra virgin olive oil

½ x quantity Maionesa (see page 245)

185 g (6½ oz) tin good-quality preserved tuna

3 sprigs curly parsley, leaves picked and chopped

Place the potatoes, carrots and eggs in a large saucepan and cover with water. Bring to the boil over medium–high heat, then reduce the heat to a simmer. Remove the eggs after 4 minutes and plunge into cold water. Peel the eggs as soon as they're cool enough to handle and roughly chop. The vegetables will take different times to cook, so keep an eye on them – you want them to be firm but not hard. When you can pierce them with a small knife or skewer with the slightest resistance they are ready. Drain and set aside to cool a little.

Boil the peas in salted boiling water for 4–5 minutes if fresh, or 2 minutes if frozen. Drain and plunge into iced water to cool down.

Peel the potatoes and carrots and cut into small chunks or cubes. Transfer to a large bowl, season with salt and white pepper and loosely dress with the vinegar and olive oil (the vegetables will better absorb the flavours when they are still warm). Allow to cool completely, then coat with the maionesa and stir through the cooked peas, tuna and chopped egg.

Garnish with the curly parsley to keep things a little retro – some institutions around Barcelona go for a full-on '70s vibe and garnish with black olives and strips of roasted red capsicum (bell pepper) to contrast the sea of milk-white mayonnaised potato.

MUSCLOS AL TIGRE

STUFFED MUSSELS

This recipe is a really interesting way to make stuffed mussels, using the mussel shell as a ready-made spoon. You can add scallops, prawns (shrimp) or any seafood or crustacean to the mix here.

This little star is served a lot at special family gatherings and around the Barceloneta neighbourhood in Barcelona, where the local bars make it as a clever way to use up left-over cooked mussels.

This recipe doubles perfectly for a larger party with friends and family.

Makes 12

2 eggs, beaten
2 tablespoons full-cream (whole) milk
150 g (5½ oz/1 cup) plain (all-purpose) flour
sourdough or panko breadcrumbs, to crumb
2 tablespoons chopped tarragon or parsley
sea salt and freshly cracked black pepper
1 litre (34 fl oz/4 cups) rice bran, grapeseed or vegetable oil, for deep-frying
lemon wedges, to serve

Mussels

250 ml (8½ fl oz/1 cup) white wine
1 fresh bay leaf
2 sprigs thyme, leaves picked and chopped
1 teaspoon peppercorns
1 kg (2 lb 3 oz) mussels, scrubbed and debearded
pinch of salt

Béchamel

500 ml (17 fl oz/2 cups) full-cream (whole) milk
1 fresh bay leaf
3 tablespoons plain (all-purpose) flour
3 tablespoons extra virgin olive oil

For the mussels, heat a large, deep frying pan or wok with a lid over high heat. Add the white wine, bay leaf, thyme and peppercorns and bring to a simmer. Add the mussels and salt, then cover and steam for 3–4 minutes, until the mussels open. Discard any mussels that remain closed.

Using a slotted spoon, remove the mussels from the pan and transfer to a bowl. Reserve the cooking liquid for the béchamel. Remove the mussels from their shells and reserve the 12 best, unbroken, equal-sized shells for filling. Roughly chop the mussel meat and set aside.

To make the béchamel, heat the milk, bay leaf and 50 ml (1¾ fl oz) of the reserved cooking liquid until it starts to steam – do not let the mixture boil. Remove the bay leaf and discard.

In another small saucepan, heat the flour and oil over low heat and stir to make a roux. Once the roux starts to sizzle and take on a sandy texture, add the warmed milk mixture and whisk rapidly to avoid lumps. Keep whisking until the béchamel becomes smooth and thick. This will take 5–7 minutes. Fold through the chopped mussels and spoon into the reserved shells. Allow to cool before placing in the fridge for at least 1 hour to set.

Set up three small bowls and place the beaten egg and milk in one, the flour in another and the breadcrumbs and herbs in the third. Season the egg wash with salt and pepper.

Once set, pass the mussels and their shells through the flour, then the egg wash and finally the breadcrumbs.

Heat the oil in a deep-fryer or large saucepan to 185–190°C (365–375°F). Drop a breadcrumb into the hot oil; if it sizzles straight away, the oil is ready.

Lower the stuffed mussels into the oil and fry for 4–6 minutes, until golden brown. Drain on paper towel and serve immediately with plenty of lemon wedges for squeezing over.

C°CA DE
RECAPTE

CATALAN PIZZA SLICE

This is Catalunya's answer to pizza, except it's rectangular and has no cheese! All generations adore this slice of convenience, which is usually made on public holidays – festivals such as Easter, La Mercé, Sant Joan, La Diada and Navidad. On these special occasions, a little sugar is often sprinkled over the top of more traditional ingredients, such as salty anchovies or sardines and smoky vegetables. 'Recapte' means a collection or harvest, and historically locals would gather produce from their gardens and take them to the village bakers who would make the 'coques' in the one oven for the entire town.

Also similar to the French pissaladière, today this popular dish is sold in local bakeries all year round and often with other, more modern toppings, such as ham and cheese, or spinach, raisins and pine nuts – a very typical Catalan combination. There's also a famous sweet variety for the festival of Coca de Sant Joan, to celebrate the summer solstice, but more the beginning of the two-month-long school summer holidays!

Eaten hot, at room temperature or cold, it's a great picnic dish for the beach, park or a trip to the mountains.

Makes 2 large or 4 small pizzas

180 ml (6 fl oz) lukewarm water
2 teaspoons dried yeast granules
2 tablespoons extra virgin olive oil
½ teaspoon caster (superfine) sugar
350 g (12½ oz) plain (all-purpose) flour, plus extra for dusting
pinch of salt

Toppings
olive oil, for brushing and drizzling
1 x quantity Escalivada (see page 34)
8 salted anchovy fillets
1 tablespoon baby capers
10 pitted black olives
1 teaspoon caster (superfine) sugar

Preheat the oven to 220°C (430°F) (fan-forced). Line a baking tray with baking paper.

Combine the water, yeast, oil and sugar in a small jug and allow to stand for 5 minutes at room temperature.

Place the flour and salt in a large bowl. Once the yeast mixture starts to froth, slowly mix it into the flour until a rough dough forms. Transfer the dough to a well-floured work surface and knead for 5 minutes, until you have a smooth, firm dough. Place the dough on the prepared tray, cover with a clean and ever-so slightly damp tea towel and leave to rest at room temperature for 15–20 minutes, until it has risen by one-third.

Divide the dough into two or four balls, depending on your preference. Working with one piece of dough at a time and keeping the remaining dough covered with the tea towel at all times, use a rolling pin to roll the dough into a rough rectangle shape, about 6 mm (¼ in) thick. Transfer to the baking tray (you may need two trays) and repeat with the remaining dough.

Brush the dough lightly with olive oil, then arrange the escalivada in alternating strips across the top in an even layer. Drape over the anchovies, followed by the capers and black olives. Sprinkle with the sugar and bake for 12–15 minutes depending on their size.

Drizzle with a little extra olive oil, cut into random pieces and eat straight off the tray.

CARGOLS PICANTS

SNAILS

You'll often find fasting snails hanging in netted bags at market delis, with their long necks swinging out through the gaps. Valencia has quite a history of cooking them as a tapas or in rice dishes – anything to get them out of 'l'hort' (the vegetable patch).

Typically known as a very French dish, it was the Romans who actually popularised eating snails throughout Europe. You can find them served across Italy, Portugal, Spain and Greece, where strictly controlled purging techniques are employed to maintain a clean, homogenised and hygienic product. You can even try your own little backyard ranch if you're keen!

Serves 4

1½ tablespoons extra virgin
   olive oil
1 onion, finely diced
5 garlic cloves, finely chopped
250 g (9 oz) fresh chorizo, diced
1 whole dried chilli
2 teaspoons tomato paste
   (concentrated purée)
60 ml (2 fl oz/¼ cup) dry
   apple cider
3 ripe tomatoes, grated, skins
   discarded
1 sprig rosemary
200 g (7 oz) tinned snails in brine,
   drained
salt flakes and freshly cracked
   black pepper
baguette, to serve

Heat the oil in a medium frying pan over medium–high heat, add the onion and cook for 5 minutes, or until beginning to soften. Add the garlic and cook for a further 5 minutes, then add the chorizo and chilli. Cook until the chorizo starts to crisp, then add the tomato paste and stir through for 3–5 minutes, until dry and beginning to brown. Add the cider and simmer for 1 minute, then add the grated tomato, rosemary sprig and snails. Season with salt and pepper and cook for 10 minutes, or until a thick sauce has formed.

Serve the snails and their sauce with ripped baguette, and any left-over cider from the bottle.

BUNYOLS DE BACALLÀ

SALTED COD FRITTERS

This is Catalunya in one mouthful! These fritters are usually eaten as a special Sunday morning tapas before the main meal. 'Bunyol' means 'badly done' or when something has not turned out as expected. A lot of great dishes in history have evolved from mistakes or errors and these little imperfect balls of perfection are a favourite in every Catalan family.

There are a few different techniques to making these balls of bacallà (salt cod). The most effective way I've found is to make them similar to a churros pastry, with eggs or a choux pastry mix for a fluffier, pillow-like result. You can make the mixture the day before, if you like.

Makes 15–20

300 g (10½ oz) prepared bacallà (salt cod) fillets (see page 28)
1 medium (200 g/7 oz) desiree or floury potato, peeled and chopped
2 sprigs thyme
2 tablespoons extra virgin olive oil
80 g (2¾ oz) plain (all-purpose) flour
2 eggs
1 garlic clove, minced
2 tablespoons chopped parsley
sea salt and ground white pepper
1 litre (34 fl oz/4 cups) rice bran, grapeseed or vegetable oil, for deep-frying
lemon wedges, to serve
Allioli (see page 244), to serve (optional)

Place the bacallà in a large saucepan and cover well with cold water. Bring to a simmer over medium heat and cook for 3 minutes, then remove from the heat and allow to sit for 10 minutes.

Remove the bacallà with a slotted spoon and set aside in a large bowl. Add the potato and thyme to the poaching liquid, return the pan to medium heat and bring to the boil. Reduce the heat to a simmer and cook the potato until soft. Strain the potato and add to the bacallà, reserving the liquid for the batter.

Bring 150 ml (5 fl oz) of the reserved cooking liquid, 150 ml (5 fl oz) water and the olive oil to the boil in a medium saucepan. Remove from the heat and gently rain in the flour, whisking to avoid any lumps, until thickened and smooth. Allow to cool slightly before whisking in each egg, one at a time, until incorporated.

Mash the potato with the bacallà as much as you can – it's fine to have a few lumps of fish. Stir through the garlic and parsley.

Return the batter to a low heat and, using a wooden spoon or spatula, fold through the bacallà and potato mixture and cook gently for 10 minutes, until a thick batter forms and starts to come away from the base and side of the pan. At this point, taste the mixture and adjust the seasoning with sea salt and a little white pepper.

Allow the batter to cool a little, then refrigerate until completely cold. This will make it easier to handle and stops the balls from sticking together when frying.

Heat the oil in a saucepan to 185–190°C (365–375°F). Drop a pinch of batter into the hot oil; if it sizzles straight away, the oil is ready.

Using two tablespoons (or smaller if you wish), form the batter into 15–20 rough balls. Carefully lower 5–6 balls into the hot oil and cook for 2–3 minutes each side, until golden. Remove the fritters from the oil and drain on paper towel, then repeat with the remaining balls. Serve with lemon wedges for squeezing over and a good dollop of allioli, if you like.

BROQUETES
DE GAMBES

PRAWN COCKTAIL SKEWERS

The pairing of crustaceans and cured ham is a cocktail party favourite around the world. The Catalans love prawn (shrimp) heads and it's quite typical to see punters at restaurants or beach shacks slurping them like straws.

Serve these as a really quick and easy summer appetiser or offer them individually as canapés at your next party and see if anyone eats them like a true Catalan!

Serves 4

2½ tablespoons extra virgin olive oil

zest and juice of ½ lemon

1 garlic clove, minced

2 teaspoons chopped parsley leaves

salt flakes and freshly cracked black pepper

8 green king prawns (jumbo shrimp), deveined, heads and tails left intact

8 thin slices jamón

8 large metal or pre-soaked bamboo skewers

oil spray

Combine the olive oil, lemon zest and juice, garlic, parsley and salt and pepper, to taste, in a bowl.

Rinse the prawns and pat dry with paper towel, then coat them in the marinade. Wrap the jamón around the middle of each prawn and slide them onto the skewers, through the tail and out the head.

Heat a barbecue or large flat grill plate to high. Spray the surface with oil and cook the prawns for 3–4 minutes each side, until the jamón is starting to crisp and the prawn flesh has turned pink.

Serve to go.

PATATES BRAVAS

SPANISH POTATOES

While not typically Catalan there is a distinct style to serving patates bravas within Catalunya. Literally meaning 'brave potatoes' they are doused in a very garlicky allioli followed by an extremely spicy red sauce. They are generally only eaten as tapas, often shared with friends or family at a street-side terrace bar. The last potato is called 'la patata de vergonya' (the shameful potato). The mere mention of this one last lonely 'brava' has the 'bravest' of the group jumping to declare their lack of shame and hastily eating what's left in the bowl.

Some bars serve fat patates bravas, whereas others prefer small and crispy potatoes, but I think a bit of both is always good; those burnt little crispy bits, which break up the warm starchy mouthfuls of potato soaked in sauce, are delicious.

Serves 4

60 ml (2 fl oz/¼ cup) extra virgin olive oil
½ onion, finely diced or grated
2 small red chillies, chopped
pinch of sea salt
2 teaspoons smoked pimentón
1 teaspoon spicy pimentón
2 teaspoons cayenne pepper
3 tablespoons plain (all-purpose) flour
1 tablespoon sherry vinegar
650 ml (22 fl oz) Brou de pollastre (see page 247) or store-bought chicken stock
5 medium sebago, king edward or russet potatoes, peeled and cut into 3–4 cm (1¼–1½ in) uneven chunks
1 litre (34 fl oz/4 cups) rice bran, grapeseed or vegetable oil
salt flakes
1 x quantity Allioli (see page 244)

Heat the olive oil in a frying pan over medium heat, add the onion, chilli and salt, then reduce the heat to low and slowly sweat the onion for 5–7 minutes, until translucent. Add both pimentóns and the cayenne and stir through well. Add the flour and cook, stirring, for 1 minute, until all the oil has been absorbed and you have a roux consistency. Add the sherry vinegar, then gradually pour in the stock, whisking continuously to avoid any lumps. Once all the stock has been added, simmer gently for 10 minutes until thickened and the flour has cooked out. Remove from the heat and blend with a hand-held blender until smooth and lump-free. Pass through a fine sieve for a perfectly silky finish.

Set aside to cool before transferring the sauce to a squeeze bottle or clean tomato sauce (ketchup) bottle.

Pat dry the potato with a clean tea towel and place in a wide-based frying pan with the rice bran oil. Make sure both the potato and oil are at room temperature.

Bring the oil to a rolling simmer over medium–high heat, stirring occasionally to prevent the starches sticking. Cook for 12–15 minutes, until the potato begins to turn golden. Using a slotted spoon, scoop out a potato chunk and make sure that it's cooked on the inside. Strain off the oil then drain the potato on paper towel. Transfer to a serving bowl and sprinkle with salt flakes.

Douse the potato in the red sauce and allioli. Dig in with small forks or toothpicks.

L'HORT

THE VEGETABLE PATCH

Seasonal vegetables dictate the home-cooked meals and 'menú del dia' (menu of the day) offerings found in restaurants throughout Catalunya. The biggest meal of the day is lunch (la comida), and Catalans will think nothing of sitting down to at least two or three courses before continuing their day or retiring for 'siesta'. Restaurants build their menus around what's in season and available at the local market, offering a soup or salad to start – depending on the time of year – a main dish and a side, finished off with dessert.

Although Catalunya is known for its high-quality fish and cured meat products, the humble vegetable still makes up the majority of the Catalan diet. Catalans take great pride in their produce, respecting the history and knowledge of cultivation, which has been passed down through the generations. The anticipated arrival of each season can be witnessed at the market. Colourful stalls spill over with an abundance of high-quality and affordable ingredients, ready for locals to buy and turn into their favourite salad, side or hero dish of the day.

Catalunya's mild Mediterranean climate is perfect for growing a wide variety of vegetables and, as such, several ingredients have been awarded the official seals, DOP (Protected Designation of Origin) or IGP (Protected Geographical Indication), recognising their unique quality. From rice grown in the Ebro Delta and olives from Les Garrigues, to the dried white ganxet beans of the Maresme and Vallès, along with calçots, potatoes, pears, clementines and hazelnuts, the revered DOP and IGP labels help to preserve and maintain the intimate connections between locality, environment and produce.

Visiting or living in Catalunya teaches you how to slow down and respect the way things grow and change, and look forward to every season to discover and understand its unique landscape and food. This chapter traverses those seasons and celebrates the fresh produce and vegetable dishes that are most prized in Catalunya.

CALÇOTS

CHARRED CATALAN SCALLIONS

The 'calçotada' is a truly unique, late wintertime, culinary Catalan custom – a cult event on the calendar year. Calçots are only grown between December and March and their harvest results in a festive gathering at a wood-fired barbecue setting under the first bursts of springtime sun.

A messy affair – bibs are worn like medals and wine is passed around in a traditional 'porró' (a glass wine pitcher drunk straight from the spout) – the long, mini leek-like, blackened scallions are wrapped tightly in porous newspaper to sweat, soften and sweeten. Traditionally served on a rooftop terracotta tile, the calçots' charred outer layers are peeled down to reveal the white, soft flesh that is then dunked into the inseparable salvitxada and, with a tilted head, lowered into the mouth.

The 'calçotada' also includes a large platter of assorted barbecued meats (see page 132) to mop up any remaining salvitxada and soak up all the over-pouring of wine!

Serves 4–6

6–8 bunches calçots (Catalan scallions), thick spring onions (scallions) or baby leeks

1 x quantity Salsa salvitxada (see page 236)

Fire up a charcoal or wood-fired barbecue 40–60 minutes before you want to start grilling. You want to get it to a point where the coals have stopped smoking and you can't hold your palm 15 cm (6 in) above the coals for more than 4 seconds without really feeling a sting.

Clean the calçots a little by cutting off the roots and washing any dirt away under running water. Trim some of the greens on top if they're very long and stringy.

Place the calçots on the grill and allow each side to char and burn gradually, turning them every 4–6 minutes, for even cooking. The calçots will start to blister out some moisture and let off a sizzling hiss when they are ready.

Wrap the calçots in plenty of newspaper for 10 minutes to sweat, sweeten and impart all that charred flavour to the flesh.

Unwrap and serve on a large platter with the salvitxada in a few bowls scattered around the table. Calçots are often eaten while standing to get a better head tilt. Avoid any white tablecloths and invite people to wear bibs – they will thank you for it!

CREMA DE CASTANYES I BOLETS

CHESTNUT & WILD MUSHROOM SOUP

This dish is autumn love in a bowl. On the streets of Barcelona, as soon as the summer sun starts going down earlier in the evenings, the chestnut and 'moniato' (sweet potato) wood-fired gallon drum stoves pop up on every corner of the Cuitat Vella (gothic quarter).

Take a walk down Les Rambles to the Mercat de La Boqueria where you will find the home of Bolets Petràs – a 50-year-old stall, specialising solely on the humble fungi. It is one of the biggest foodie tourist attractions in the entire city.

Serves 4–6

1 kg (2 lb 3 oz) chestnuts
120 g (4½ oz) butter
2 tablespoons extra virgin olive oil
1 medium leek, white part only, thinly sliced
1 turnip, swede (rutabaga) or parsnip (about 250 g/9 oz), peeled and diced
2 litres (68 fl oz/8 cups) vegetable stock, heated
100 ml (3½ fl oz) pouring (single/light) cream
salt flakes and freshly cracked black pepper
200 g (7 oz) assorted mushrooms, such as pine, saffron caps, chestnut, king brown, Swiss brown and button, thickly sliced
2 garlic cloves, thinly sliced (or young garlic shoots if you can find them)
2 sprigs thyme
60 ml (2 fl oz/¼ cup) dry cooking sherry

Preheat the oven to 180°C (350°F) fan-forced.

Using a small serrated knife, score the top of each chestnut with a cross. Transfer to a wire rack set over a roasting tin and roast for 20 minutes, or until they begin to split open.

Transfer the chestnuts to a large heatproof bowl and cover tightly with plastic wrap to steam for 10 minutes. Peel the nuts and set aside, discarding the shells.

Heat half the butter and 1 tablespoon of the oil in a large heavy-based saucepan over medium heat. Add the leek and a pinch of salt and cook, stirring occasionally, for 4–6 minutes, until soft. Add the peeled chestnuts, your root vegetable of choice and stir to coat, then pour in the vegetable stock. Increase the heat to high and bring to a high simmer for 20 minutes, until the liquid has reduced by one-third. Reduce the heat, then carefully purée using a hand-held blender. Simmer the soup for a little longer if you prefer a thicker result.

Remove from the heat and strain through a fine sieve to remove any raw chestnut pieces. Whisk through the cream and season to taste.

Heat the remaining olive oil and 1 teaspoon of the remaining butter in a frying pan over medium–high heat. Add the mushrooms and cook, stirring, until sizzling. Add the garlic and thyme and cook for 4–6 minutes, until the mushrooms are soft and any liquid has reduced down. Add the sherry and reduce by half. Remove from the heat and immediately stir through the remaining butter.

Divide the soup among bowls and top with the sautéed mushrooms.

CARXOFES
A LA CATALANA

CATALAN ARTICHOKES

If you fly into Barcelona's El prat airport in late spring and catch the train through the Delta del Llobregat, you'll spot a sea of blooming perennial artichokes by the roadside among the yellow flowering fennel. They're a big part of the local landscape no matter how much Barcelona sprawls and they emit a calming, grounding vision after the hustle of the busy airport.

Artichokes that are simply sliced and deep-fried, with or without a batter, are a big bar favourite in Catalunya. I like to really make a meal of them and add some complementary staple Catalan friends – starring the raisin and the pine nut! Any dish you see on a menu that ends in 'a la Catalana' usually means it will involve these two ingredients, both typically grown and produced just south of Barcelona.

You can serve this dish as a side to a simple pan-fried fish fillet or roast chicken, as an entrée or as a star on its own with crusty bread and extra virgin olive oil.

Serves 4

6–8 artichokes, hard outer leaves removed

2 lemons

1½ tablespoons extra virgin olive oil

1 thick slice speck, pancetta, or bacon, roughly chopped (optional)

¼ fennel bulb, sliced, fronds reserved

2 celery stalks, sliced into chunks

2 garlic cloves, smashed

1 fresh bay leaf

2 tablespoons raisins

80 ml (2½ fl oz/⅓ cup) dry sherry or white wine

200 g (7 oz) baby spinach leaves

1 tablespoon pine nuts, toasted

1 teaspoon salt flakes

Trim the stalks from the artichokes, leaving 4–5 cm (1¾–2 in) of stalk attached and peel the outer layer. Cut the artichokes in half and remove any choke fibres from the middle. Transfer to a large bowl filled with cold water and the juice of ½ lemon.

Heat the oil in a large frying pan with a lid or a wide saucepan over medium–high heat. Add the speck, pancetta or bacon and fry until the fat has rendered and the pork is just beginning to crisp. Strain the artichokes and add to the pan, along with the fennel, celery and garlic and lightly sauté for 2 minutes. Add the bay leaf and raisins and stir to combine, then add the sherry or white wine. Reduce the heat to medium–low, cover and cook for about 8 minutes, or until the liquid has reduced by half. Remove the lid and squeeze in the juice of 1 lemon.

Continue cooking to reduce as much liquid as you like, making sure the artichokes are soft and a knife slips through the stalks easily by the end of cooking (add more wine or water if necessary).

Remove from the heat and gently stir through the baby spinach leaves and the juice from the remaining lemon half. Transfer to a large serving platter and scatter the pine nuts, reserved fennel fronds and salt flakes over the top.

AMANIDA DE TºMÀQUETS

TOMATO SALAD

There's a tiny bar down by the port of Barcelona called La Plata, where they serve this tomato salad to accompany their signature dish of fried 'pescadito' (freshly caught anchovies). This dish is all about simplicity and the quality of your ingredients – the acid will wash down any fried accompaniment you want to use here orwork as a stand-alone salad using locally grown tomatoes and a really good-quality sherry vinegar. It can really quench your summer thirst.

Serves 4

1 white onion, sliced
400 g (14 oz) super-ripe heirloom tomatoes, roughly chopped and sliced
2 teaspoons salt flakes
2 tablespoons dried Greek or Mexican oregano
125 g (4½ oz/½ cup) Arbequinas casolanes (see page 25) or small wild olives
2 tablespoons sherry vinegar
60 ml (2 fl oz/¼ cup) extra virgin olive oil
crusty rustic bread, to serve

Plunge the onion into iced water and set aside for 5 minutes. Drain.

Arrange the tomato in a large serving dish and sprinkle over the salt flakes and oregano.

Scatter the olives and onion over the top and drizzle with the vinegar and olive oil.

Serve with crusty, rustic bread and a side of Sardines a la graella (see page 90), if you like.

ESPÀRRECS BLANC I MIMOSA

WHITE ASPARAGUS

Spring is the time for these delicately grown spears. Catalunya has a long history of growing and appreciating the unique white asparagus, which is hidden away from the sun its entire life. Dotted throughout Catalunya, but especially around the Municipality of Gavà, you'll see piled-up dirt mounds blanketing and protecting the pearl-white stems and tips.

Due to their delicate nature, white asparagus are often cooked in a 'blanc' first of boiling water, flour and lemon juice, then cooled down rapidly and served simply and just below room temperature to admire their earthy flavour.

Serves 4

16–20 white asparagus spears (tinned or jarred are OK)
1 tablespoon plain (all-purpose) flour
1 teaspoon lemon juice
1 teaspoon sea salt
3 sprigs parsley
1 tablespoon olive oil
1 thick slice sourdough bread, ripped into small breadcrumbs
1 teaspoon chopped tarragon leaves
pinch of sea salt
1 x quantity Salsa almadroc (see page 235)
extra virgin olive oil, to drizzle
2 hardboiled eggs, whites and yolks separated
purple micro herbs, such as mustard cress or radish (optional)

Trim 2–3 cm (¾–1¼ in) off the woody ends of the asparagus. Prepare the 'blanc' by combining the flour, lemon juice, salt, parsley and 2 litres (68 fl oz/8 cups) water in a wide saucepan. Bring to the boil, then reduce the heat to a gentle simmer and blanch the asparagus for 8–10 minutes, depending on their thickness. Strain and set aside in iced water.

Heat the olive oil in a small frying pan over medium heat. Add the breadcrumbs and fry until crisp and golden, then transfer to a small bowl and sprinkle with the tarragon and a pinch of salt.

Spoon the salsa almadroc into a serving bowl and arrange the asparagus on top. Drizzle some extra virgin olive oil over the spears, then finely grate the egg whites and yolks over the asparagus. Scatter with the breadcrumbs and micro herbs, if using, and serve straight away.

AMANIDA DE FAVETES I PÈSOLS

BABY BROAD BEAN & PEA SALAD

Catalans love, love, love their broad (fava) beans! So hardy and easy to grow, they set up the vegetable garden for the rest of the summer's plantings by fixing much-needed nitrogen in that deliciously rich Catalan soil.

Inspiration for the flavour combinations in this dish comes from one of my favourite restaurants, Can Fabes – owned by three-Michelin star chef Santi Santamaria, who has since sadly passed away – located in the beautiful broad bean-growing lands of Sant Celoni, situated between the Montseny and Montnegre massifs. My favourite meal was an aspic-like jelly packed full of teeny-tiny, bright green podded baby broad beans with the mild, fresh essence of ginger. So clean and unforgettable.

If you can find it in a deli, finely shaved duck jamón, tossed through at the end, dresses up this salad beautifully.

Serves 4

500 ml (17 fl oz/2 cups) vegetable stock
½ bunch tarragon
200 g (7 oz) fresh or frozen podded broad (fava) beans
150 g (5½ oz) fresh or frozen podded peas
2 mint sprigs, leaves thinly sliced
sea salt and freshly cracked black pepper
3 tablespoons extra virgin olive oil
1 tablespoon sherry vinegar
1 teaspoon freshly grated ginger
juice of ½ lemon
¼ radicchio, shredded
100 g (3½ oz) queso fresco or firm ricotta

Bring the vegetable stock and two tarragon sprigs to the boil in a medium saucepan over medium–high heat.

Blanch the broad beans for 2 minutes then, using a slotted spoon, remove from the stock and immediately transfer to a bowl of iced water. Remove the outer skins of most of the larger beans, leaving the smaller ones intact for a touch of bitterness.

Bring the stock back to the boil and blanch the peas for 4 minutes, then strain and cool in the iced water.

Finely chop the remaining tarragon leaves and place in a medium bowl with the blanched broad beans and peas, mint, a pinch of salt and pepper and half the olive oil.

In a separate bowl, combine the vinegar, ginger, lemon juice and remaining oil, then toss through the shredded radicchio. Mix this through the broad bean and pea mixture.

Transfer the salad to a serving platter and dot the queso fresco or ricotta over the top.

CIGRONS
AMB BLEDES

SAUTÉED CHICKPEAS & SILVERBEET

Chickpeas (garbanzo beans) were brought to Catalunya by the Andalucians, which were introduced to them by the Moors and Phoenicians. Today, you can buy cooked legumes in large refrigerated tubs at markets and shops around Catalunya, just as you'd buy the dried versions at home. This recipe shows you how to cook dried chickpeas but, if you're short on time, tinned chickpeas will work just as well here.

Serves 4 as a side

200 g (7 oz) dried chickpeas (garbanzo beans), soaked overnight or 1 x 400 g (14 oz) tin chickpeas, rinsed and drained

3 garlic cloves, 2 slit up one side, 1 finely chopped

2 fresh bay leaves

2 tablespoons extra virgin olive oil

1 brown onion, finely diced

1 teaspoon fennel seeds

½ cinnamon stick

1 teaspoon ground allspice

1 bunch silverbeet (Swiss chard), stems separated from leaves, both roughly chopped

185 ml (6 fl oz/¾ cup) vegetable stock

2 lemons

salt flakes and freshly cracked black pepper

If using dried chickpeas, drain and place them in a large saucepan with twice the amount of water, the slit garlic cloves and the bay leaves. Bring to the boil over medium–high heat and cook for 50–70 minutes (larger and older chickpeas will take longer to cook). Drain and discard the garlic and bay leaves. Skip this step if using tinned chickpeas.

Heat the oil in a large frying pan over medium–high heat. Add the onion and cook for 6 minutes, or until beginning to soften. Add the finely chopped garlic, fennel seeds, cinnamon and allspice and stir well to combine.

Add the sliverbeet stems and vegetable stock to the pan and cook for 4–5 minutes, then add the chickpeas and the juice of 1 lemon. Continue to cook, until the chickpeas are heated through, then season to taste and mix in the silverbeet leaves until just wilted.

Transfer to shallow bowls, squeeze over the remaining lemon and sprinkle with some extra cracked pepper.

PATATES DE POBRE

PEASANT'S POTATOES

Poor man's potatoes! This rich dish is the number one favourite Catalan accompaniment to any grilled meat, fish or poultry. It all depends on the quality of the potatoes, so use the very best you can find.

Serves 4

125 ml (4 fl oz/½ cup) extra virgin olive oil
1 kg (2 lb 3 oz) Dutch cream potatoes, peeled and sliced about 3 mm (⅛ in) thick
1 brown onion, sliced into rounds
3 garlic cloves, slit down one side
1 green capsicum (bell pepper), sliced
170 ml (5½ fl oz/⅔ cup) vegetable or chicken stock, heated
salt flakes and freshly cracked black pepper

Heat the oil in a wide heavy-based saucepan over medium–high heat. Add all the ingredients to the pan and give everything a stir.

Reduce the heat to medium–low, cover and cook for 6–8 minutes. Remove the lid and keep cooking until the oil has been absorbed by the potato and the potato is cooked through (add a little extra water if necessary to prevent the potato burning too much and sticking to the base of the pan).

Season to taste and serve straight away with your choice of meat, fish or poultry.

SAMFAINA

RATATOUILLE

This is the Catalan version of Spanish pisto or French ratatouille, and it turns summer garden vegetables into a finely balanced taste of the Mediterranean. It is usually served with bacallà (salt cod) or grilled fish.

Serves 4

1 medium eggplant (aubergine), cut lengthways into 3 cm (1¼ in) thick slices

3 teaspoons sea salt

4 ripe tomatoes

60 ml (2 fl oz/¼ cup) extra virgin olive oil

2 red onions, thickly sliced

½ teaspoon ground white pepper

3 garlic cloves, thinly sliced

1 fresh bay leaf

2 sprigs thyme

2 small zucchini (courgettes), sliced into 3 cm (1¼ in) thick rounds

1 red capsicum (bell pepper), cut into 3 cm (1¼ in) chunks

½ green capsicum (bell pepper), cut into 3 cm (1¼ in) chunks

1 yellow capsicum (bell pepper), cut into 3 cm (1¼ in) chunks

2 teaspoons tomato paste (concentrated purée)

pinch of saffron

1 tablespoon sherry vinegar

salt flakes and freshly cracked black pepper

Place the eggplant in a colander with a bowl underneath and toss with 2 teaspoons of the salt. Stand for 20 minutes, then rinse under cold water and pat dry with paper towel.

Score a cross in the base of each tomato. Bring a medium saucepan of salted water to the boil and blanch the tomatoes for 30–40 seconds, until the skins start to peel away from the flesh. Drain and plunge the tomatoes into iced water. Peel off the skins and discard, then pat the tomatoes dry with paper towel and cut into quarters. Discard the seeds and roughly chop the flesh.

Heat 2 tablespoons of the olive oil in a large frying pan over medium heat and add the eggplant. Fry for 5 minutes, turning frequently, until golden on all sides, then set aside on a plate. Add the remaining oil, the onion, remaining salt and the white pepper to the pan and cook, stirring occasionally, for 10 minutes. Add the garlic, bay leaf and thyme and cook for a further 2–3 minutes until the onion is soft.

Add the zucchini and cook for 5 minutes, then add the capsicums. Add 125 ml (4 fl oz/½ cup) water and keep cooking and stirring everything together for about 5 minutes, until the mixture starts to brown and stick to the base of pan. Stir through the tomato paste until it starts to darken in colour, then add the chopped tomato, saffron, vinegar and another 125 ml (4 fl oz/½ cup) water. Return the cooked eggplant to the pan and reduce the heat to medium–low. Cover and cook for 10–15 minutes, until the vegetables have cooked down to a chunky sauce-like consistency.

Check the seasoning, then remove from the heat and transfer to a serving bowl. Season with salt flakes and freshly cracked black pepper and serve.

TRINXAT

PYRENEES BUBBLE & SQUEAK

This dish comes from the mountainous principality of Andorra, where their official language is Andorran Catalan. Much like the Irish colcannon, 'trinxat' is perfect in the Catalan winters where cabbages grow well after a little frost.

'Trinxat' meaning 'chopped', traditionally has three parts to its creation – boiling the potato and cabbage, mashing everything together, then forming a potato hash-like cake with a little help from some pork fat, to give it a lovely firm crust on each side. It goes particularly well with pork cutlets or a fried egg.

Serves 4 as a side

½ green cabbage, quartered, dark green outer leaves discarded
500 g (1 lb 2 oz) desiree potatoes, peeled, halved if very large
sea salt
1 teaspoon white peppercorns
150 g (5½ oz) piece pancetta or speck, cut into short strips
2 garlic cloves, minced
2 tablespoons extra virgin olive oil
salt flakes and freshly cracked black pepper

Place the cabbage and potato in a large stockpot and cover with cold water. Season well with sea salt and the white peppercorns, then bring to the boil and cook for about 40 minutes, until tender. Drain well and set aside to cool a little. Cut and discard the core from the cabbage and squeeze as much water out of the leaves as possible. Spread the cabbage leaves and potato out on a large clean tea towel and allow to steam-dry.

Cook the pancetta or speck in a large non-stick frying pan over medium heat until crisp.

Reduce the heat to as low as it can go and return the cabbage and potato to the pan. Mash using a large potato masher to remove any remaining moisture. Stir through the garlic and olive oil until everything is pasted together – a few lumps and strings of cabbage are ok. Season, to taste and serve.

If you would like to turn the potato and cabbage into a large potato hash, squash the mixture down and out to the side of the pan after stirring through the garlic and olive oil. Curve a spatula around the edge of the pan to help define the shape, then cook for 6–8 minutes, until the base is golden and brown. Place a large plate over the top and invert the compressed hash onto the plate. Return to the pan and crisp up the other side. Serve on a large plate and cut into wedged portions.

TRENCAT DE CEBA AMB COL ESCABETXADA

SMASHED ONION SALAD WITH PICKLED CABBAGE

The town of Figueres is famous for the Salvador Dalí museum and the sweet pink onions that grow in the local area. In fact, the whole Alt Empordà and Baix region is synonymous with the international culinary world, being home to the famous restaurant El Bulli. The area spans the Costa Brava all the way up to the Pyrenees and is a concentrated and well-respected cultural wine route, too.

The winter 'Tramuntana' winds of Alt Empordà are said to stir up artistic creativity, cleansing the skies to cast the light. The constant, unescapable noise of rattling windows and smashing shutters are said to push people's minds to the limit!

The technique used here to bruise the onion reminds me of these clamorous winds and I have made this dish quite colourful to reflect the intense shades of Dalí's surrealist skies from the Alt Empordà. Enjoy!

Serves 4

¼ red cabbage, cut into large, bite-sized chunks
1½ tablespoons sea salt
160 g (5½ oz) caster (superfine) sugar
250 ml (8½ fl oz/1 cup) white wine vinegar
1 fresh bay leaf
8 black peppercorns
4 whole allspice
6 pink onions, red salad onions or purple shallots, peeled
4–6 radishes, sliced
1½ tablespoons extra virgin olive oil
2 tablespoons micro herbs, such as sorrel or baby beetroot (beets) (optional)

Toss the cabbage in the salt and let stand for 30 minutes. Rinse well and completely dry with paper towel, then transfer to a large glass jar or non-reactive bowl.

Set aside two teaspoons of the sugar and tip the rest into a small saucepan. Add the vinegar, bay leaf, peppercorns, allspice and 60 ml (2 fl oz/¼ cup) water and bring to a simmer. Cook until the sugar is dissolved, then remove from the heat and set aside to cool. Once completely cool, pour over the cabbage and refrigerate.

Chop the onions into quarters or six chunks if really large. Place in a clean tea towel and, using a rolling pin or the base of a glass bottle, bruise the chunks to break them slightly and release some of their juice. Transfer to a medium bowl and sprinkle with the remaining sugar and a pinch of salt. Set aside for 5 minutes, then plunge into iced water and drain.

Remove two large handfuls of the cabbage from its pickling liquid (any left over can stay in the 'escabetx' and be used another time) and place in a medium bowl with the onion, radish and olive oil. Mix well to combine.

Divide the salad among plates and sprinkle with a few micro herbs, if desired.

LA
COSTA
THE COAST

The dramatic coastline of Catalunya starts at the Pyrenees on the French border and travels down the western Mediterranean Sea to the province of Valencia. From wild seascapes and seemingly undiscovered shorelines, to the more commercial package-tourism of the Costa Brava in the north or Costa Daurada in the south, there is something for everyone along this diverse stretch of the Iberian Peninsula.

Catalans love the beach and will happily spend their time walking, bathing, taking part in sporting activities, dining, going to a 'xiringuito' (local beach bar) or visiting quaint historical medieval fishing towns to appreciate the white-washed architecture and art history. Having access to such a diverse coastline inevitably means access to fresh seafood and Catalunya is blessed with some of the best fish and shellfish in the world. As a result, these ingredients are ingrained in the Catalan diet and feature daily on restaurant menus and in home kitchens. Fish of every colour, shape and size are proudly displayed at markets, where locals clamour to buy the catch of the day to take home and turn into something delicious, but always simple, to let the quality of the fish and 'taste of the sea' speak for themselves.

Catalunya also has a great tradition of preserving seafood and the world's best tinned tuna, anchovies, mackerel and sardines come from this region. Another integral Catalan ingredient is 'bacallà' (salt cod) and you will find it throughout the province in salads, stews or as a standalone dish served simply with patates (potatoes).

The concept of 'mar i muntanya' (sea and mountain), or perhaps the more affectionate term 'surf and turf', is distinctly Catalan, and it's this union of high-quality seafood and meat in local dishes that underlines the true essence of Catalan cuisine, and has awarded Catalunya its rightful place on the culinary world stage as a gastronomic giant. To truly understand the Catalan kitchen is to grasp this marriage of landscapes through its produce.

CLOÏSSES AMB CAVA I JAMÓN

CLAMS IN CAVA & JAMÓN

The D.O. status of Cava meaning 'cave' or 'cellar' was created to distinguish it from French Champagne (colloquially called 'Xampany' in Catalunya). The majority of Spain's cava is made from the dominant white grape varieties of the Penedès region, which spans Baix Penedès on the Mediterranean Sea where the climate is warm, through to the low-lying hills of the central Penedès and up to the higher, inland area of Superior (Alt) Penedès, where the temperature drops significantly and humidity increases.

This dish is a perfect representation of the diverse 'mar i muntanya' (sea and mountain) culture, where cured ham complements fresh clams, which are then married together by Catalunya's proud Cava sparkling white wine.

Razor clams instead of clams are also a strong tradition for this combination.

Serves 4

3 tablespoons olive oil
60 g (2 oz) salted butter
1 large brown onion, finely diced
3 sprigs thyme
4 garlic cloves, sliced
12 slices jamón, torn
350 ml (12 fl oz) Cava or dry
   sparkling white wine
2 tablespoons plain (all-purpose)
   flour
1.5 kg (3 lb 5 oz) clams (vongole),
   soaked for 1 hour to remove any
   sand and grit
2 tablespoons chopped parsley
crusty bread, to serve

Heat the oil and half the butter in a medium heavy-based saucepan over medium heat. Add the onion and thyme and cook for 6 minutes, or until the onion is soft. Add the garlic and jamón and sauté for 2 minutes, then add the Cava. Whisk in the flour and bring the sauce to a boil. Add the clams, cover tightly with a lid and cook for 6–8 minutes, until the clams open. Toss in the remaining butter with the parsley and swirl the pan to coat.

Serve the clams and the juices from the pan in a large bowl with fresh crusty bread on the side. Alternatively, toss through some cooked spaghetti to make a substantial dinner.

SARDINES A LA GRAELLA

CHARCOAL SARDINES

Outdoor barbecue 'festes' (festivals) are a regular feature at household gatherings and in villages where 'a sardinada' (grilled sardine party) is the main event. Locals might gather in the town square to celebrate a patron saint and the council will put on a big feast of sardines for everyone to enjoy, play a little 'rumba Catalana' and maybe dance the traditional 'sardana'.

The sardines are cooked covered in fig leaves to help steam them along and curb some of the fishy aroma! They're then used as a biodegradable plate to serve them on.

This dish goes particularly well with a tomato salad (see page 66) in summer or on top of the Coca de recapte on page 44.

Serves 4

12–16 sardines, gutted and rinsed, patted dry with paper towel
10 fresh fig leaves (from a neighbour's tree if you're lucky), slightly dampened so they don't ignite in flames
30 g (1 oz/¼ cup) golden raisins, roughly chopped
80 ml (2½ fl oz/⅓ cup) sherry or red wine vinegar
1 garlic clove, sliced
2 tablespoons capers
3 tablespoons extra virgin olive oil
peel of ¼ orange
1 teaspoon brandy
salt flakes and freshly cracked black pepper
2 tablespoons pine nuts, toasted

Fire up a charcoal or wood-fired barbecue 40–60 minutes before you want to start grilling. You want to get it to a point where the coals have stopped smoking and you can't hold your palm 15 cm (6 in) above the coals for more than 4 seconds without really feeling a sting.

Place the sardines on a grill over the coals, cover with the fig leaves and cook for 4–6 minutes, until the bottom of the fish is charred. Remove the leaves and turn the sardines over, then cover again and cook for a further 4–6 minutes.

Meanwhile, heat the raisins, vinegar, garlic and 2 tablespoons water in a small saucepan over low heat for 4–6 minutes, until the raisins have absorbed the water. Remove from the heat and set aside in a medium heatproof bowl to cool. Add the oil, orange peel and brandy, and season with salt and pepper. Mix through until you have a vinaigrette consistency.

Place the fig leaves on a large serving platter and top with the sardines. Drizzle with the raisin and caper sauce and sprinkle over the toasted pine nuts.

CALAMARS FARCITS DE PORC I BOLETS

CALAMARI STUFFED WITH PORK & MUSHROOM

You'll find many stuffing combinations for calamari in Catalunya and they all beautifully pair the flavours of land and sea. Mushrooms are sometimes used instead of minced (ground) meat or prawns and chorizo might be mixed with fresh herbs and spinach; you can even stew the stuffed calamari in a rich sauce for a deeper flavour. This is a simple, lighter version of the dish but the triple dose of umami really reminds me of those Catalan flavours. I also like to add a little Vietnamese fish sauce to the mix to give it some extra saltiness from the sea.

Serves 4

800 g (1 lb 12 oz) whole calamari
1 shallot, finely diced
2 garlic cloves, finely chopped
1 field mushroom, finely chopped
20 g (¾ oz) dried black trumpet
   fungi, rehydrated in boiling
   water for 10 minutes, drained
   and finely chopped
200 g (7 oz) minced (ground) pork
1 tablespoon fish sauce
50 g (1¾ oz) jamón, finely diced
¼ bunch chives, finely chopped
½ teaspoon ground white pepper
3 tablespoons extra virgin olive oil
125 ml (4 fl oz/½ cup) white wine
1 lemon
1 tablespoon butter, softened
green salad leaves, to serve

Separate the tentacles from the calamari hoods by gently pulling them off and remove the transparent bone from the centre of the calamari. Thoroughly rinse the inside of the hoods under running water until completely clean but leave the skin and flaps attached. Cut away the beaks and ink sacs and rinse the tentacles. Alternatively, you can ask your fishmonger to do this for you. Set aside.

Combine the shallot, garlic, mushrooms, pork, fish sauce, jamón, chives, white pepper and 1 tablespoon of the oil in a large bowl. Loosely stuff each calamari hood with the mixture, making sure not to overfill the calamari as the cases will shrink. Thread a toothpick through the top of the calamari to prevent the stuffing from spilling out. Set aside on a tray.

Heat the remaining oil in a large frying pan over medium heat, add the calamari and fry for 5–6 minutes on each side. Prick each tube several times with a toothpick or skewer to release some of the juices and continue cooking for a further 10–12 minutes, turning to get an even golden seal on the outside. Throw the tentacles in the pan in the last 3 minutes of cooking to soak up the remaining pan juices.

Transfer the calamari and tentacles to a chopping board and rest for 6 minutes before slicing the stuffed calamari.

Meanwhile, pour the wine into the pan with the zest and juice of half the lemon and simmer with any remaining pan juices for 5 minutes. Add the butter in the last minute of cooking and swirl to combine.

Divide the stuffed calamari and tentacles among plates and drizzle the sauce from the pan over the top. Cut the remaining lemon half into wedges and serve with the calamari and green salad leaves on the side.

MUSCLOS
AMB XORIÇO

MUSSELS WITH CHORIZO

Mussels are our economical friends from the sea, yet this meal impresses no matter the cost. I made Karen Martini's version of this dish when I worked at her restaurant Cala Bonita in Ibiza, and it was the number one bestseller that summer.

I like to chargrill the tomatoes to take me back to the good times of that summer: campfires on the beach, eating mussels straight from the pot and scooping up all the goodness from the pan using the mussel shell as a shovel.

Serves 4–6

150 g (5½ oz) fresh chorizo
4 roma (plum) tomatoes
1 tablespoon extra virgin olive oil
4 shallots, cut into quarters
4 garlic cloves, chopped
2 sprigs tarragon
250 ml (8½ fl oz/1 cup) dry white wine
125 ml (4 fl oz/½ cup) dry sherry
1.5 kg (3 lb 5 oz) mussels, scrubbed and debearded
4 thick slices sourdough bread, chargrilled

Remove the chorizo from its casing and set aside.

Heat a barbecue or large flat grill plate to high. Char the tomatoes until the skins begins to blacken and shrink away from the flesh. Remove from the heat and, once cool enough to handle, remove and discard the skins and roughly chop the flesh into chunks. Set aside in a bowl.

Heat the oil and chorizo in a large stockpot, frying pan or wok over high heat. Cook, stirring and breaking up the chorizo with a wooden spoon, for 5 minutes, until crispy. Add the shallot and cook for 5 minutes, then add the garlic and stir to combine. Add the chopped tomato, tarragon, white wine and sherry, bring to the boil and cook for 8–10 minutes, until slightly reduced. Tip the mussels into the pot and mix them around to coat in the sauce. Cover and steam, shaking the pot from side to side every so often, for 6–8 minutes, until the mussels have opened. Discard any mussels that do not open.

Toss well to lift up all the chorizo that's gravitated to the bottom of the pan and serve in the pot on the table with the chargrilled bread and plenty of serviettes and finger bowls.

ESCABETX
DE VERAT

MACKEREL
ESCABECHE

Catalunya has a long history of pickling and preserving good-quality fish and meat. Now famous, these products are often expensive and prized throughout the region and further afield. The sweet and sour method used in this recipe lends itself to the stronger flavours of game birds, such as pheasant, partridge, pigeon and quail, and oily fish, such as sardines, tuna, bonito, salmon and trout – even eel works well. The fish gently absorbs the acid while it cools and preserves, which really mellows out the intense flavour and gives it a satisfying depth of flavour.

Serves 4

4 x 200 g (7 oz) small mackerel, filleted (you can also use sardines or an 800 g/1 lb 12 oz side of Spanish mackerel, cut into 4 fillets)
145 ml (5 fl oz) extra virgin olive oil
sea salt
12 Dutch carrots, peeled, tops trimmed, thicker ones sliced in half lengthways
½ fennel bulb, sliced
2 shallots, thickly sliced whole
2 garlic cloves, halved, germ removed
2 fresh bay leaves
2 sprigs thyme
10 pink peppercorns
10 white peppercorns
½ teaspoon coriander seeds
½ teaspoon sweet pimentón
125 ml (4 fl oz/½ cup) sherry or red wine vinegar
½ teaspoon caster (superfine) sugar
crusty baguette or rye bread, to serve
horseradish cream, to serve (optional)

Heat a medium non-stick frying pan over high heat. Drizzle the mackerel with 1 tablespoon of the oil and sprinkle with a little salt, then add to the pan and seal for 1 minute on each side.

Heat 60 ml (2 fl oz/¼ cup) of the oil in a medium saucepan over medium heat and add the carrot, fennel, shallot, garlic, bay leaves, thyme, peppercorns and coriander seeds. Gently cook for 5–6 minutes, until the vegetables just start to soften. Remove from the heat and stir through the pimentón, vinegar, ½ teaspoon of salt and the sugar.

Transfer the mackerel to a heatproof dish and pour over the vegetables and warm 'escabetx' marinade to cover the fish. Stand at room temperature for a minimum of 2 hours for the vinegar flavours to penetrate the fish before serving or, even better, leave to cool for 20–30 minutes, then refrigerate overnight and serve the following day.

Serve at room temperature with a crusty baguette or on rye bread as an aperitivo. A little dollop of horseradish cream on top is also special.

RAP AMB CARXOFES I TOMÀQUET

MONKFISH & ARTICHOKES WITH TOMATO CONCASSE

This is more of a dinner-party dish or something you might find at a good-quality Catalan institution. For me, this combination of sea, mountain and vegetable garden encapsulates the Catalan landscape itself. Monkfish and baked whole artichokes stuffed with concasse tomatoes (a French technique that removes the skins and seeds and chops the flesh into perfect little dice) beautifully showcases Catalunya on a plate, and particularly the Garraf coastline. This interpretation is inspired by the dedicated chefs at the Gran Hotel Rey Don Jaime in the coastal town of Castelldefels, where I worked for two years perfecting my Catalan hospitality knowledge.

Serves 4

80 ml (2½ fl oz/⅓ cup) extra virgin olive oil
4 garlic cloves, chopped
2 sprigs thyme
4 tomatoes
4 slices jamón, finely chopped
salt flakes and freshly cracked black pepper
4 globe artichokes, hard outer leaves removed, stems trimmed
juice of 2 lemons
125 ml (4 fl oz/½ cup) dry white wine
375 ml (12½ fl oz/1½ cups) Brou de pollastre (see page 247) or store-bought chicken stock
4 x 200 g (7 oz) skinless monkfish fillets
1 tablespoon butter
2 teaspoons finely chopped parsley leaves

Preheat the oven to 190°C (375°F) fan-forced.

Combine the olive oil, garlic and thyme in a small bowl and set aside.

Score a cross in the base of each tomato. Bring a medium saucepan of salted water to the boil and blanch the tomatoes for 30–40 seconds, until the skins start to peel away from the flesh. Drain and plunge the tomatoes into iced water. Peel off the skins and discard, then pat the tomatoes dry with paper towel and cut into quarters. Discard the seeds and dice the flesh into small even-sized pieces. Transfer to a bowl and combine with the jamón and half the garlic oil. Season with salt and pepper.

Trim the stalks from the artichokes, leaving 4–5 cm (1¾–2 in) of stalk attached and peel the outer layer. Cut the artichokes in half and remove any choke fibres from the middle. Transfer to a large bowl filled with cold water and the juice of 1 lemon.

Place the artichokes in a baking dish and evenly spoon the tomato and jamón mixture into the centre of each artichoke, pushing the mixture in so it doesn't fall out. Pour the white wine and stock into the base of the dish, cover with foil and bake for 25–30 minutes, until the artichoke stalks are soft when pierced with a knife.

Meanwhile, cut away any sinewy bits from the monkfish.

Heat the remaining garlic oil in a large frying pan over medium–high heat and seal the fish on both sides for 2–4 minutes, until golden. Uncover the artichokes, place the fish on top and bake in the oven for 8–10 minutes, until cooked through.

Place a monkfish fillet and two artichokes on each plate. Stir the butter through all the juices in the baking dish, then add the parsley and remaining lemon juice. Season with salt and pepper and drizzle over the fish and baked artichokes. Serve immediately.

SUQUET DE PEIX

CATALAN FISH STEW

This dish is a very typical household soupy stew, using a little bit of this and that left over from the fishermen's catch in one big hotpot wonder.

It can get quite fancy in restaurants and on special occasions, with all kinds of shellfish, such as scampi and cockles or baby squid and scallops, or even lobster. This recipe is a simple, relatively inexpensive version perfect for making at home.

Serves 4

2 tablespoons extra virgin olive oil

3 garlic cloves

3 ripe tomatoes, grated, skins discarded

2 teaspoons tomato paste (concentrated purée)

1 teaspoon sea salt

400 g (14 oz) Dutch cream potatoes, peeled and sliced into 5 mm (¼ in) thick rounds

125 ml (4 fl oz/½ cup) dry cooking sherry

about 400 ml (13½ fl oz) Fumet de peix (see page 246) or store-bought fish stock

pinch of saffron

½ teaspoon sugar

1 tablespoon brandy

2 tablespoons Picada (see page 237)

4 x 180 g (6½ oz) trevally, king fish or hake cutlets

200 g (7 oz) firm white fish fillets, such as monkfish, blue eye, rock ling or flathead, cut into 4–5 cm (2½–2 in) chunks

8 large green prawns (shrimp), peeled and deveined, heads and tails left intact

8 mussels, scrubbed and debearded

crusty bread, to serve

Heat the oil in a medium–large heavy-based cast-iron pan over medium heat. Add the garlic, tomato, tomato paste and salt and cook, stirring occasionally, for 10 minutes or until beginning to darken in colour and reduced. Add the potato, sherry, stock, saffron and sugar and give everything a good stir. Cover and simmer for 15 minutes, making sure the potato is fully submerged in the liquid – you may need to add a little more stock depending on the size of your saucepan.

Remove the lid, add the brandy and stir through the picada, then poke the fish pieces into the stew. Cook for 4–6 minutes, then add the prawns and mussels and cook for 2–3 minutes, until just cooked through and opened. Discard any mussels that do not open.

Serve the stew on the table in its pot with plenty of bread for mopping up all the delicious juices.

PEIX A LA SAL

SALT-BAKED FISH

This well-loved cooking technique involves enveloping a whole fish in a thick layer of salt, which forms a crust as it cooks, allowing the fish to steam inside while imparting a gentle salt flavour. Once cooked, you crack the crust to reveal a dish that is incredibly sweet and juicy every time. This dish goes particularly well with Patates de pobre (see page 74) and Samfaina (see page 76).

Serves 4

1.2 kg (2 lb 10 oz) seasonal whole fish, such as coral trout, snapper, bream or sea bass, gutted and cleaned (ask your fishmonger to do this for you)
1 tablespoon extra virgin olive oil
1 lemon, sliced
1.5 kg (3 lb 5 oz) coarse rock salt
2 sprigs thyme
2 fresh bay leaves
10 white or black peppercorns
4 egg whites
Patates de pobre (see page 74) and Samfaina (see page 76), to serve

Preheat the oven to 190°C (375°F) fan-forced.

Wash and dry the fish very well with paper towel, then rub the fish all over with the oil. Stuff the inside of the fish with the sliced lemon.

Blitz the salt, thyme, bay leaves and peppercorns in a blender. Transfer to a large bowl and mix in the egg whites and 3 tablespoons water.

Spread half the salt mixture on a large flat baking tray and place the fish on top. Cover with the remaining salt slurry and press the salt firmly around the fish to make an even layer with no gaps. Bake for 20 minutes, or until the crust begins to brown and harden.

Remove the fish from the oven and let stand for 10 minutes. Crack the salt layer and gently scrape all the salt away from the fish. Peel away and discard the skin, along with the lemon.

Starting at the head, make a slit down the top edge of the fish to the tail and another along the middle of the fish, from neck to tail. Release the head and, using a spatula, follow the bone line and lift out the first fillet starting in the middle and edging outwards towards the top. Detach the remaining fillet and transfer the fish to a serving platter. Gently lift the fish skeleton from the tail upwards to reveal the flesh. Make another cut down the centre of the fish and lift each fillet away from the skin onto the serving platter.

Serve with patates de pobre and samfaina.

ARRÒS NEGRE

BLACK RICE

The 'socarrat' that forms on the base of a paella while the rice is cooking is always the hero. It's this caramelised, crusty blanket that keeps you digging back for more.

This dish is a must served with Allioli (see page 244), which really makes this dramatic-looking dish come to life on the plate. Most connoisseurs of the arròs negre will mix allioli through their entire portion to coat it evenly, but I like to dip every mouthful into my garlicky mayonnaise blob and then drown it in plenty of freshly squeezed lemon.

Serves 4

3 tablespoons extra virgin olive oil
2 garlic cloves, smashed open
2 red bullhorn peppers (if in season) or 1 red capsicum (bell pepper), thinly sliced
1.2 litres (41 fl oz) Fumet de peix (see page 246) or store-bought fish stock
pinch of saffron
3 x 8 g (¼ oz) sachets squid ink
420 g (15 oz/1½ cups) Sofregit (see page 241)
250 g (9 oz) whole cuttlefish or calamari, cleaned and rinsed, hoods cut into diamonds or squares, tentacles set aside
150 g (5½ oz) small or medium peeled prawns (shrimp), roughly chopped
400 g (14 oz) medium-grain rice, such as bomba or calasparra (supermarket medium-grain rice will suffice here, but you'll notice the difference if you can track down the real thing)
80 ml (2½ fl oz/⅓ cup) dry sherry or white vermouth
300 g (10½ oz) clams (vongole) or pipis, soaked for 1 hour to remove any sand and grit
8 scampi
salt flakes
Allioli (see page 244), to serve
lemon wedges, to serve

Heat the oil in a 32–34 cm (12½–13¼ in) paella pan or frying pan over medium heat. Add the garlic and bullhorn pepper and cook, stirring occasionally, for 6–8 minutes, until the pepper is soft and its colour has run out into the oil. Transfer the pepper to a plate and set aside, leaving the garlic in the pan.

Meanwhile heat the stock in a medium saucepan over medium heat and stir through the saffron and squid ink.

Add the sofregit and cuttlefish hoods to the paella pan and heat until sizzling. Cook, stirring frequently, for 5 minutes, then add the prawns and rice. Stir to coat the rice grains evenly, then pour in the sherry or vermouth and fold through until everything is really well combined.

Add half the stock to the pan and spread out the mixture, so it's in an even layer. Gently simmer over low heat for 6 minutes, shaking the pan back and forth every so often to loosen and aerate the rice.

When half the liquid has been absorbed, create a few little holes in the mixture using the handle of a wooden spoon to help prevent the rice from burning. You don't want to stir the mixture at this stage as this will disrupt the 'socarrat' base and over-activate the starches in the rice. Each grain of rice needs to stay individual.

Rotate the pan around the burners on the stovetop if you see there isn't an even heat, so each side of the pan cooks evenly. Once the liquid has completely evaporated, place the clams or pipis and cuttlefish tentacles on top of the rice, then pour in the remaining stock. Cook for a further 6 minutes, giving the pan a little shake from time to time. When reduced by half again, add the scampi and red pepper and simmer for another 6 minutes, until the rice has absorbed all but a thin layer of liquid on top. Check the seasoning and add a little salt if necessary. The texture of the rice should be just al dente.

Remove from the heat, cover with newspaper (ink on ink!) or a clean (dark-coloured) tea towel and set aside for 6–8 minutes to settle and absorb the remaining liquid.

Serve with allioli and lemon wedges, and don't stop until it's gone.

BACALLÀ A LA LLAUNA

SALT COD FROM THE PAN

Salt cod – what a fish! It's one of most popular ingredients used in traditional Catalan dishes. Brought down by the Basques from the Atlantic, today it's mostly fished in Iceland and Canada and now travels the globe. 'Bacallà a la llauna' directly translates as 'cod in a tin', referring to the roasting tin it's cooked in. Its simplicity means that this dish is heavily dependent on the quality of your bacallà.

These days you can buy ready-to-go bacallà as pre-soaked fillets at major seafood suppliers or Mediterranean delicatessens. If you have time you can also make your own with black cod or a similar-fleshed fish by completely burying it in rock salt and leaving it for two days in the refrigerator. Brush and rinse away the salt and soak the fish in cold water for 30–40 minutes. It will then be ready to use. For this recipe I've used traditional bacallà that just needs to be soaked at home.

Serves 4

1 x 800 g (1 lb 12 oz) bacallà
35 g (1¼ oz/¼ cup) plain
   (all-purpose) flour
200 ml (7 fl oz) light-tasting extra
   virgin olive oil
4 garlic cloves, sliced
1½ tablespoons sweet pimentón
250 ml (8½ fl oz/1 cup) dry
   white wine
½ teaspoon salt flakes
¼ bunch parsley, chopped
green salad leaves or Patates de
   pobre (see page 74), to serve

To prepare the bacallà, place the fish in a glass or ceramic dish and cover with cold water. Set aside in the fridge and change the water every 4 hours, three or four times depending on how salty you like it and how thick the bacallà is. When you're happy with the flavour of the fish, pat it dry with paper towel, then cut into four equal-sized portions and pat dry again.

Preheat the oven to 170°C (340°F) fan-forced.

Coat the bacallà in the flour and dust off any excess.

Heat the oil in a large frying pan over medium–low heat. Add the bacallà and gently cook for 10–12 minutes on each side until just golden brown. Lower the heat if the oil starts to sputter – you want to poach the fish rather than fry it, so it's important to keep the oil temperature below 100°C (210°F). Transfer the bacallà to a roasting tin or ovenproof dish.

Reduce the heat and, in the same oil, fry half the garlic for 2 minutes until beginning to brown, then add the pimentón quickly followed by the wine. Allow to simmer for 6–8 minutes, until the alcohol has evaporated and the mixture has reduced slightly.

Pour the sauce over the bacallà and bake for 10 minutes.

Pound the remaining garlic slices with the salt flakes using a mortar and pestle, then combine with the parsley. Spoon this mixture over the bacallà just before serving.

Serve with green salad leaves or patates de pobre.

ARRÒS PARELLADA

RICH MAN'S RICE

Known as rich man's rice, this dish is designed to be eaten with the finest silverware! This famous recipe was named after a prominent Catalan 'bon vivant' lawyer who was a habitual client at the now defunct Restaurant Suís on La Plaça Reial just off Les Rambles. As so happens from time to time at restaurants with regular customers, diners soon have their favourite table set aside for them, they always order the same thing and always tip the same amount. This dish, which contains no shells, bones or skins from the fish, was likely a result of refining the lawyer's favourite meal into a more polite way of eating it in front of his lunch guests, which was brusquely followed by an 'I'll have what he's having' moment.

Serves 4

2 tablespoons extra virgin olive oil
1 red capsicum (bell pepper), finely diced
100 g (3½ oz) pork loin, sliced into 1 cm (½ in) strips
2 pork sausages, sliced into 1 cm (½ in) rounds
200 g (7 oz) skinless boneless chicken thighs, cut into 2–3 cm (¾–1¼ in) chunks
100 g (3½ oz) monkfish or rock ling fillet, cut into 2–3 cm (¾–1¼ in) chunks
4 artichoke hearts in brine, drained and halved
250 ml (8½ fl oz/1 cup) white wine
pinch of saffron
12 mussels, scrubbed and debearded
280 g (10 oz/1 cup) Sofregit (see page 241)
1 x 100 g (3½ oz) calamari hood, cleaned and rinsed, finely diced
400 g (14 oz) short-grain rice, such as bomba or calasparra
200 g (7 oz) prawns (shrimp), peeled and deveined
1 litre (34 fl oz/4 cups) Fumet de peix (see page 246) or store-bought fish stock, heated
100 g (3½ oz) romano (flat) beans, cut into 3 cm (1¼ in) pieces

Heat the olive oil in a large 32–34 cm (12½–13¼ in) paella pan or frying pan over medium heat, add the capsicum and sauté for 8–10 minutes, until soft and its colour has run out into the oil. Remove the capsicum from the pan and set aside on a small plate. Add the pork, sausages, chicken, monkfish or rock ling and artichoke to the pan and cook until golden all over, stirring and rotating the pan for even cooking. Remove from the pan and set aside on a large plate.

Meanwhile, bring the white wine, saffron and 125 ml (4 fl oz/½ cup) water to the boil in a large saucepan. Throw in the mussels, then cover and steam until opened. Remove from the heat, discard any mussels that do not open and, when cool enough to handle, remove the mussels from their shells. Set the flesh aside in the mussel liquid.

Add the sofregit and calamari to the paella pan over medium–high heat and cook, stirring, for 5 minutes. Add the rice and stir to coat in the sofregit, then add the prawns, the reserved meat, fish and artichoke and three-quarters of the stock. Stir everything together while the mixture comes to the boil.

Once boiling, reduce the heat to low and, without stirring, gently simmer for 10 minutes. Rotate the pan around the burners on the stovetop if you see there isn't an even heat, so each side of the pan cooks evenly. Pour in the remaining stock, add the beans and gently shake the pan from side to side and check the bottom with a spoon if you fear it may be catching. Reduce the heat to very low if it is burning and don't disturb the mixture too much as you want a nice 'socarrat' crust to form on the base. Continue to simmer, until all but a thin layer of liquid remains on the surface, then pour the mussels and their liquid and the capsicum over the top of rice.

Remove from the heat, cover with a clean tea towel and let the mixture sit for 6–8 minutes to absorb any remaining liquid. Divide among shallow bowls and serve.

ROSSEJAT

FIDEOS PASTA PAELLA

'Rossejat', meaning 'browned' involves toasting pasta noodles before combining with a sofregit base and adding flavours of the sea. Although called a paella, its cooking technique more closely resembles that of a pilaf.

This dish is said to have been invented at sea by fishermen who had run out of rice and substituted the short, thin noodles picked up over the Mediterranean Sea in Corsica or Sardinia. Brought onto shore where Catalunya borders Valencia, this region is now home to the classic 'fideuà' – a pasta dish that mimics all the rich shellfish contents of the famous Valencian seafood paella.

Serves 4

300 g (10½ oz) fideos, angel hair short-cut pasta or spaghettini, cut into 5 cm (2 in) lengths
3 tablespoons extra virgin olive oil
2 garlic cloves, smashed
1 red capsicum (bell pepper), cut into short thin strips
1 litre (34 fl oz/4 cups) Fumet de peix (see page 246) or store-bought fish stock
1 fresh bay leaf
pinch of saffron
1 teaspoon sea salt
280 g (10 oz/1 cup) Sofregit (see page 241)
300 g (10½ oz) whole cuttlefish or calamari, cleaned and rinsed, hoods finely diced (or minced in a blender), tentacles set aside
150 g (5½ oz) small peeled prawns (shrimp)
8 large green prawns (shrimp)
Allioli (see page 244), to serve
lemon wedges, to serve

Toast the fideos with 2 tablespoons of the olive oil and one garlic clove in a 32–34 cm (12½–13¼ in) paella pan or frying pan over medium–high heat. Keep moving the pasta around the pan with a wooden spoon or spatula for 8–12 minutes, until evenly toasted and golden. Transfer to a large plate in a single layer and set aside.

Reduce the heat to medium, add the remaining oil and the capsicum and cook, stirring occasionally, for 8–10 minutes, until soft and its colour has run out into the oil. Transfer the capsicum to a small plate.

Meanwhile, heat the stock, bay leaf, saffron and salt in a saucepan over medium heat until simmering.

Preheat the oven to 180°C (350°F) fan-forced.

Add the sofregit to the paella pan and heat until sizzling, then add the cuttlefish or calamari. Cook for 5 minutes, add the small prawns and stir through for 2 minutes, then add the toasted fideos. Stir to coat well, then add the cuttlefish or calamari tentacles and the warmed stock and shake the pan gently to evenly distribute the fideos.

Reduce the heat to low and simmer for 10 minutes, until three-quarters of the liquid has evaporated. Place the large prawns on top, then transfer the pan to the oven for 12 minutes and watch the fideos spike up towards the heat!

Serve with allioli and lemon wedges.

TONYINA A LA PLANXA

TUNA STEAK

There's a long history of tuna fishing in Catalunya where blue fin, yellow fin, long fin and bonito are eaten fresh or turned into high-quality preserved tuna in tins or bottles. The 'ventresca' (tuna belly) is particularly sought after and it is sometimes tinned separately and sold at a higher price. Fresh tuna steaks are always around the markets, especially in the summer months when the bigger-sized fish come in to bite. They're a great-quality protein to take home and cook up as is: simple, fresh and cooked medium–rare.

Serves 4

1 kg (2 lb 3 oz) russet, king edward or sebago potatoes, washed and cut into 1 cm (½ in) thick chips (fries)

625 ml (21 fl oz/2½ cups) light-tasting extra virgin olive oil

4 x 200 g (7 oz) tuna loin steaks

sea salt and freshly cracked black pepper

Alberginia i nous (see page 234), to serve

lemon wedges, to serve

Preheat the oven to 160°C (320°F) fan-forced.

Pat the potato chips dry with paper towel.

Heat all but 2 tablespoons of the oil in a large saucepan over medium–high heat. To test if the oil is ready, dip the end of a chip in and wait for it to sizzle. Fry the chips in two batches for 5–6 minutes each, allowing the oil to come back up to temperature before adding the next batch. Remove with a slotted spoon and transfer to a baking tray lined with paper towel to absorb the oil. Evenly spread the chips out on baking trays with a comfortable space between each chip. Transfer to the freezer (yes freezer, it stops them cooking and also holds the outside surface starch in) for 10–15 minutes.

Bring the oil back up to temperature, then fry the chips in batches again, placing each cooked batch in the oven to keep warm before cooking the next, for a further 5–6 minutes, until golden.

Lightly rub the remaining oil into the tuna steaks and season with salt and pepper. Heat a large frying pan or chargrill pan over medium–high heat and cook the tuna for 3–6 minutes each side, depending on how pink you like it and how much you trust your fishmonger! Remove from the heat and transfer to individual serving plates.

Serve the tuna steaks with the chips and the alberginia i nous, plus lemon wedges on the side.

PELAIES AL FORN

WHOLE BAKED FISH

Buying fish whole is very popular in Catalunya. You can see how fresh it is, choose your size and use the head and bones for stock, even after it's been cooked. This well-travelled provincial dish originates from the French–Catalan coastline and is a go-to weeknight meal for a lot of families, as it's easy to prepare with no time locked over the stovetop and very little washing up.

Serves 4

1 lemon, halved
60 ml (2 fl oz/¼ cup) extra virgin olive oil
4 sprigs tarragon, leaves and stalks separated
1½ teaspoons fennel seeds, lightly toasted
1 teaspoon ground white pepper
sea salt
1.6–1.8 kg (3½ lb–4 lb) whole flat fish, such as flounder, sole, halibut or John Dory, gutted and cleaned (ask your fishmonger to do this for you)
4 medium desiree potatoes, unpeeled, sliced into 5 mm (¼ in) thick rounds
1 fresh bay leaf
60 ml (2 fl oz/¼ cup) Fumet de peix (see page 246), store-bought fish stock or water
2 tablespoons anise liqueur, such as pernd, grappa or ouzo
4 shallots, halved
1 green capsicum (bell pepper), thickly sliced into rounds
4–6 small vine-ripened tomatoes, halved
salt flakes and freshly cracked black pepper

Preheat the oven to 200°C (400°F) fan-forced.

In a spice grinder, blender or mortar and pestle, blitz or pound the peel and juice of half the lemon, 2 tablespoons of the olive oil, the tarragon leaves, toasted fennel seeds, white pepper and 1 teaspoon of sea salt until you have a chunky pesto-like paste.

Score 3–4 incisions across the fish on each side. Rub the herb paste on both sides of the fish and set aside for the flavours to infuse.

Place the potato, remaining olive oil, tarragon stems, bay leaf, fish stock, anise liqueur, shallot and a pinch of salt in a large baking dish. Give everything a good mix with your hands, then cover with a lid or foil and bake for 10 minutes.

Remove the dish from the oven and arrange the capsicum and tomato in the dish. Place the marinated fish on top and bake for 25–30 minutes, until the skin begins to shrink and fall away from the flesh.

Squeeze the remaining lemon half over the fish and season well with salt and pepper. Serve immediately.

EL CAMP

THE C○UNTRYSIDE

Catalunya's 'el camp' (countryside) is home to forests, mountains and lakes, as well as monasteries, cathedrals, castles and Roman ruins. Set against this backdrop is a strong rural heritage where passionate artisans abound: cheesemakers, charcuterie producers, bakers, farmers, winemakers and chefs, all striving to keep the flavours, traditions and techniques of Catalan cuisine alive.

After the manufacturing boom at the start of the 20th century, and then in the wake of the Spanish Civil War in the 1950s and '60s, there was a huge depopulation of rural villages all over Catalunya. Thankfully, new generations are now returning to the countryside, looking to lead a more relaxed life with their families and reignite the customs and practices that once sustained the peasant community. Foraging for local herbs or wild mushrooms in autumn is again popular, and these local ingredients have reclaimed their rightful place in the unique Catalan culinary landscape, while helping to maintain the memory of how we used to live and dine and share.

The Catalan interior landscape is diverse and whether as a tourist visiting for the first time or a born-and-bred local, there is always something to discover. Take a day trip to one of Catalunya's 'masías' (old country homesteads) and spend several hours over a long lunch immersing yourself in the local produce, or venture to one of the eleven protected wine regions to sample wine made from the local grape varieties Garnacha and Carignan, or the famous Cava, Spain's own sparkling wine.

Goat, pig and poultry farming prevail in Catalan agriculture, but it is the traditional practice of curing that makes up most of what comes out of the hills and valleys of inland Catalunya. 'Embotits' (charcuterie) come in myriad shapes, sizes, textures and flavours and appear in restaurants, supermarkets and on kitchen benchtops throughout the province. Simply placed between bread or presented on a platter, Catalan charcuterie is some of the best in the Mediterranean.

PATÉ DE PORC

PORK LIVER PÂTÉ

This rustic Catalan pâté is more of a chunky, spreadable terrine. It's superb matched with the Smashed onion salad with pickled cabbage salad on page 82 or just some crunchy bread and your favourite pickles.

In France, you might find this pâté wrapped in bacon, neatly packed into a rectangular mould and sold in slices at markets. South of the Pyrenees, however, you'll get a much more country-style peasant approach with a no bells, no whistles, down-to earth, hearty offering.

Serves 6–8

450 g (1 lb) free-range pork livers, cleaned and trimmed of sinew, diced into 3 cm (1¼ in) chunks
600 ml (20½ fl oz) full-cream (whole) milk
50 g (1¾ oz) butter
150 g (5½ oz) bacon rashers (slices), rind removed, finely chopped
2 garlic cloves
2 shallots, finely diced
½ teaspoon ground allspice
¼ teaspoon ground cloves
¼ teaspoon freshly grated nutmeg
1 teaspoon sea salt
½ teaspoon ground white pepper
1 tablespoon brandy
2 tablespoons dry sherry
2 eggs
75 g (2¾ oz) stale bread, crusts removed
450 g (1 lb) boneless pork shoulder, finely chopped
freshly cracked black pepper
8 fresh bay leaves
boiling water
crusty bread, to serve
pickles, to serve

Rinse the pork liver really well under cold water. Soak in 500 ml (17 fl oz/2 cups) of the milk and refrigerate for 1 hour. Drain the livers and discard the milk.

Preheat the oven to 100°C (210°F) fan-forced.

Melt the butter in a medium frying pan over medium–high heat and add the bacon, garlic and shallot. Give everything a stir, add the spices and salt and pepper and stir again to combine. Cook for 1 minute, then pour in the alcohol and simmer until reduced by one-third. Remove from the heat, allow to cool slightly, then place in a food processor with the livers and process to combine. Add the eggs, bread and remaining milk and process for a further 1 minute, until everything comes together. Transfer the mixture to a large bowl and fold through the chopped pork. Season with salt and pepper.

Spoon the mixture into two 400 ml (13½ fl oz) ramekins (or ovenproof clip top jars), leaving a 2–3 cm (¾–1¼ in) gap at the top, then press two bay leaves into each ramekin to decorate. Wrap the ramekins in two layers of plastic wrap to tightly seal and transfer to a deep roasting tin. Fill the tin with boiling water three-quarters of the way up the sides of the ramekins, cover with a sheet of baking paper and two layers of foil and tightly seal. Cook for 1 hour or to a core temperature of 65°C (150°F), using a kitchen thermometer to assist you.

Remove the ramekins from the roasting tin and set aside to cool, then transfer to the fridge to cool completely. Top the pâtés with the bay leaves and return to the fridge to completely set.

Serve with crusty bread and your favourite pickles.

EMBOTITS

CURED MEATS, CHARCUTERIE & SMALLGOODS

'Embotits' are cooked or cured Catalan smallgoods. There are 17 officially recognised cured sausage/salami varieties in Catalunya and the largest culture of fermenting meats comes from the 'Plana de Vic', which is home to the quintessential town of Vic. Catalan pride and support for independence is strong here and lives on through the mythical status of the sausage!

Surrounded by the Sub-Pyrenees and granite mountain range of Montseny, the valley has its own microclimate, as cool air is trapped on the low-lying plain by warmer air above, resulting in heavy fogs. This clean, cold air is perfect for pig farming and developing an excellent meat to fat ratio for making charcuterie.

A favourite and daily way to eat 'embotits' is by way of the 'entrepan' (bocadillo in Spanish) meaning 'between bread'. Catalans have a huge sandwich-eating culture: toasted or grilled, rubbed with tomatoes (see page 22) or served with simple charcuterie, cheeses, egg or tinned tuna, Catalans fill their baguettes with pride. Eaten for morning or afternoon tea, a light lunch, quick dinner or late at night, you will always find 'entrepans' sold throughout Catalunya.

Here are some typical 'embotits', some of which you may have to travel to Catalunya to find.

CURED: meats that are cased and dried to specific times, temperatures and humidity.

Fuet – made with ground (minced) pork, back fat and white pepper, this thin, slightly sweet-tasting sausage is bright white in appearance from the Penicillin-mould wash and is soft in texture and bite.

Llonganisses – quality lean pork salami ground with black peppercorns and slow-cured.

Jamón – not traditionally Catalan, but on everyone's daily shopping list.

Xoriç – a type of llonganissa made with minced (ground) pork loin and pimentón. There are spicy (picante) varieties, too.

Sobrassada – from the neighbouring island of Mallorca, this cured sausage is more like a spread or paste with added pimentón.

BOILED: meats that are cased and boiled or steamed, then cooled.

Botifarra negre – pork pancetta ground with pigs' snouts and blood.

Botifarra blanca – minced (ground) pork and fat with egg sometimes added.

Bull (blanc i negre) – head, heart, tongue and liver minced with spices and shaped into round sausages using casings from the large intestine.

Bisbe (blanc i negre) – meaning 'bishop', this sausage is made from whole tongue pieces and pigs' blood sausage.

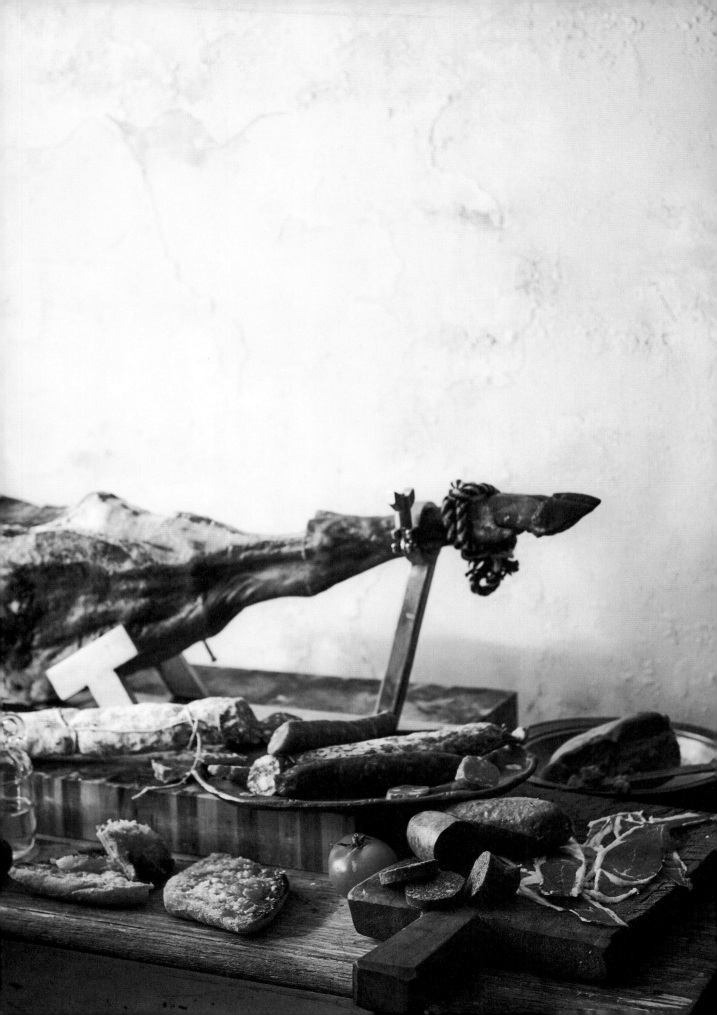

MAND⦿NGUILLES
AMB SEPIA

MEATBALLS
WITH
CUTTLEFISH

This surf and turf dish demonstrates the rich and diverse landscape of Catalunya in one pot. It is the essence of Catalan cuisine, where produce from the mountains meets those from the sea. This style of cooking, which stretches from the Pyrenees to the Costa Brava, spilling over into neighbouring Valencia where the world-famous paella 'mixta' was born, was perhaps devised not from creative genius but out of necessity. It's said that fishermen and farmers traded local produce instead of currency and that these ingredients eventually ended up in the one pot due to a lack of refrigeration.

Serves 6

250 g (9 oz) day-old sourdough bread, crusts removed, torn into small chunks
80 ml (2½ fl oz/⅓ cup) full-cream (whole) milk
200 g (7 oz) free-range minced (ground) pork
500 g (1 lb 2 oz) minced (ground) veal
280 g (10 oz/1 cup) Sofregit (see page 241)
1 egg
½ bunch chives, finely chopped
2 tablespoons extra virgin olive oil
1 brown onion, diced
2 garlic cloves, crushed
2 tablespoons tomato paste (concentrated purée)
60 ml (2 fl oz/¼ cup) anise liqueur, such as pernod, grappa or ouzo
1 large cuttlefish or calamari, cleaned and rinsed, roughly chopped into 3 cm (1¼ in) pieces
4 vine-ripened ripe tomatoes, chopped
1 star anise
375 ml (12½ fl oz/1½ cups) Brou de pollastre (see page 247) or store-bought chicken stock
Patates bravas (see page 52) or green salad leaves, to serve

Soak the bread in the milk in a small bowl for 5–10 minutes. Squeeze as much milk out of the bread as possible and discard the milk.

Combine the pork and veal mince, sofregit, egg, chives and soaked bread in a large bowl and season with salt and pepper. With wet hands, roll the mixture into golf ball-sized balls.

Heat a large frying pan over medium–high heat, add the meatballs and cook, swirling the pan to help keep the balls in an even shape, for 6–8 minutes, until coloured. Remove from the heat and transfer to a plate.

Add the olive oil and onion to the pan and cook for 8–10 minutes, until the onion is soft. Stir through the garlic and cook for a further 2 minutes, then add the tomato paste. Keep stirring, pour in the anise liqueur and simmer until evaporated, then add the cuttlefish and continue to cook until the mixture starts to colour. Stir through the tomato and star anise and bring to a simmer. Add the chicken stock, then reduce the heat to low, cover and cook for 20–30 minutes, until the cuttlefish is tender.

Add the meatballs to the pan and continue to cook for 6–8 minutes, until heated through.

Serve with patates bravas in winter or green salad leaves in summer.

CARN A LA BRASA

MIXED GRILL

A good mixed grill is often served as the main course after a 'calçotada' (see page 58), but don't let that stop you making this outside of calçot season. On the outskirts of Barcelona, you can find makeshift kitchen huts with huge outdoor grills, plastic outdoor furniture, chequered tablecloths, a 'porrón' (pitcher) full of shandy set in the middle of the table and a few local dogs hanging around being shooed away with the same set of tongs used to flip the local 'botifarra' (sausages). Groups of friends or families often make a day of it, travelling on the train from Barcelona to feast together for a long, messy lunch.

Serves 4

2 medium potatoes, halved

2 artichokes or zucchini (courgettes), halved

1 x 300 g (10½ oz) veal cutlet

4 chicken or rabbit marylands (leg quarters)

4 lamb cutlets (caps left on)

4 pork and fennel sausages

2 black puddings

1 large cured chorizo

2 fresh chorizos

2 red bullhorn peppers or red capsicums (bell peppers), halved, seeds removed

3 tablespoons extra virgin olive oil

salt flakes

Allioli (see page 244), to serve

Salsa salvitxada (see page 236), to serve

Fire up a charcoal or wood-fired barbecue 40–60 minutes before you want to start grilling. You want to get it to a point where the coals have stopped smoking and you can't hold your palm 15 cm (6 in) above the coals for more than 4 seconds without really feeling a sting.

Place all the vegetables and meats on a large tray and lightly cover with the oil.

Place a grill over the coals and put the potato halves and artichoke or zucchini in a moderately hot spot. They should start to colour up nicely after 10 minutes. You may need to move them around the grill until you find the perfect place.

Now find the hottest part of the grill and cook the veal cutlet and chicken or rabbit for 10–12 minutes each side, then move to the side of the grill, away from the coals to rest.

Place the lamb, sausages, black puddings and chorizos on the grill over an even heat and cook for 6–8 minutes. Remove anything that cooks more quickly and set aside on a baking tray in a warm spot near the barbecue to rest. You can always give it a blast at the end before serving.

Finally, add the peppers or capsicums and cook, turning three or four times for about 6 minutes each side, until the skins starts to colour and wrinkle.

Sprinkle the meats and vegetables with salt flakes and cut the veal cutlet and cured chorizo into four thick slices. Halve the fresh chorizos and black puddings and serve everything up on a large serving platter with plenty of allioli and salvitxada.

FRICANDÓ DE VERDELLA

BEEF FRICASSEE

This recipe is an adaptation of the French fricassee, except the Catalans only make it with beef or veal and serve it with an umami-rich mushroom sauce. You'll always find this on the local 'menú del dia' (menu of the day) in autumn with hand-cut chips (fries).

The foraged moixernons mushroom is the traditional choice for this recipe, but feel free to curate your own mushroom mix using different shapes, textures and aromas that are available to you. I make it differently every time! I've recently started adding a teaspoon of dark miso to anything mushroom-laden lately and, in this dish, it brings me closer to those umami and salty Catalan flavours.

Serves 4

4 dried porcini mushrooms
110 g (4 oz/¾ cup) plain (all-purpose) flour
sea salt and freshly cracked black pepper
800 g (1 lb 12 oz) skirt or flank steak (or veal rump steak), cut into 1 cm (½ in) thick slices
60 ml (2 fl oz/¼ cup) extra virgin olive oil
1 brown onion, sliced
3 garlic cloves, crushed
2 sprigs thyme
250 ml (8½ fl oz/1 cup) dry white wine
3 tomatoes, halved and grated, skins discarded
2 teaspoons dried oregano
1 teaspoon dark miso paste
600 ml (20½ fl oz) Fons fosc de carn (see page 248) or store-bought beef or veal stock
150 g (5½ oz) portobello mushrooms, sliced
150 g (5½ oz) small button mushrooms
150 g (5½ oz) oyster or shiitake mushrooms
1 x quantity Picada (see page 237)
1 litre (34 fl oz/4 cups) vegetable oil
4 medium potatoes, cut into 2 cm (¾ in) thick chips (fries)

Rehydrate the porcini mushrooms in a small bowl of boiling water for 15 minutes. Drain and set aside.

Flour and season the steak and dust off any excess.

Heat half the olive oil in a large frying pan over medium–high heat and, working in batches, seal the steak on both sides, until a thin golden crust forms. Transfer to a plate and set aside.

Add the remaining oil and the onion to the pan and cook, stirring frequently, for 6–8 minutes, until the onion starts to soften. Add the garlic, one thyme sprig and a pinch of salt and continue cooking until the onion starts to turn golden, then add the wine, grated tomato and oregano. Cook for 10–15 minutes, until most of the liquid has evaporated and the tomato starts to darken a little, then stir through the miso and add the meat back to the pan, along with the stock. Bring to a simmer, then reduce the heat to medium–low and add all the mushrooms. Simmer for 8–10 minutes, until the sauce has reduced and thickened and the meat is tender. Stir through the picada.

Meanwhile, heat the vegetable oil in a large frying pan over medium heat and shallow-fry the chips, turning frequently, for 16 minutes or until golden brown and cooked through. Drain on paper towel and sprinkle with sea salt.

Divide the steak and mushroom sauce among plates and serve with the chips to dip into all that mushroom goodness.

ESPATLLA DE XAI AL FORN

OVEN-ROASTED LAMB SHOULDER

Catalan families often eat this dish a couple of times during the Christmas period, kicking off on 8 December and carrying on through to Three Kings' Day on 6 January. It's sometimes served as a late-night dinner on the 'Nit de Nadal' (good night) or Christmas Eve. It's not complete without potatoes and picada might be spooned over the top as well. If you'd like to try something different, add a pinch of saffron to the picada recipe on page 237 and spoon over the lamb shoulder just before serving instead of the herbs.

Serves 4

500 g (1 lb 2 oz) rock salt
2 sprigs rosemary
2 fresh bay leaves
1 cinnamon stick, halved
8 juniper berries
2–2.5 kg (4 lb 6 oz–5½ lb) lamb
   shoulder, bone in
1 tablespoon extra virgin olive oil
1 teaspoon freshly cracked
   black pepper
125 ml (4 fl oz/½ cup) sherry
   vinegar
125 ml (4 fl oz/½ cup) dry
   white wine
2 garlic bulbs, cut in half crossways
2 lemons, halved
500 g (1 lb 2 oz) chat (baby)
   potatoes
1 teaspoon salt flakes
mixed fresh herbs, such as mint,
   dill, parsley, basil and tarragon
   leaves, to serve

In a blender, blitz the salt, one rosemary sprig, one bay leaf, half the cinnamon and the juniper berries until evenly chopped.

Place the lamb in a large baking dish and rub with the salt mix to coat. Set aside in the fridge for 2 hours.

Preheat the oven to 230°C (445°F) fan-forced.

Rub the salt off the lamb and rinse well. Pat dry with paper towel and allow to air-dry on a wire rack at room temperature for 30 minutes.

Smear the lamb with the olive oil and sprinkle with the pepper. Place the lamb and the wire rack on top of a baking dish and pour the vinegar, wine and 1 litre (34 fl oz/4 cups) water into the base of the dish. Throw in the garlic, two lemon halves and the remaining rosemary, bay leaf and cinnamon. Roast for 30 minutes, then remove from the oven and turn the shoulder over. Reduce the temperature to 150°C (300°F) and return the lamb to the oven and roast for a further 30 minutes. Remove, turn the lamb over again and place the potatoes in the baking dish. Return to the oven for another 30 minutes. Keep an eye on the liquid and add a little more water if the baking dish is dry and the potatoes are starting to burn. Finally, increase the heat back to 230°C (445°F), turn the lamb shoulder one last time and roast for 15 minutes.

Transfer the lamb and potatoes to a large serving dish. Squeeze the remaining lemon halves over the potatoes and sprinkle with the salt. Scatter the herbs over the lamb and serve.

GUATLLE AMB RAÏM

QUAIL WITH WINE GRAPES

In George Orwell's *Homage to Catalonia* he describes how peasants would sit in the long grass at night and mimic the sounds of female quails in order to catch the males. Today, the glut of wine variety grapes at the end of the summer happily coincides with the quail migration season and so the excess, over-ripened fruit are paired with this game bird that's often caught feeding on chicken grain at vineyard acreages.

Serves 4

4 large quail, cleaned and gutted
4 large vine leaves, soaked in cold
    water for 1 hour
12 thin slices flat pancetta
3 tablespoons extra virgin olive oil
sea salt and freshly cracked
    black pepper
2 tablespoons honey
400–500 g (14 oz–1 lb 2 oz) bunch
    fresh muscatel grapes (or other
    wine-making grape variety)
1 tablespoon butter
2 onions, thinly sliced
3 sprigs thyme
4 thick slices sourdough
1 garlic clove, peeled
125 ml (4 fl oz/½ cup) dry
    white wine
250 ml (8½ fl oz/1 cup) grape juice

Preheat the oven to 180°C (350°F) fan-forced. Line a baking tray with baking paper.

Pat the quail dry with paper towel and place a vine leaf over each bird's breast. Wrap three slices of pancetta across the breast of each quail and tuck the ends around the back. Secure with toothpicks. Rub the quail with half the olive oil and season with salt and pepper.

Heat a large frying pan over medium–high heat and brown the quail on each side until the pancetta starts to turn golden. Set aside on the prepared tray. Drizzle the remaining oil and the honey over the grapes and place on the baking tray with the quail.

Melt the butter in the frying pan over medium–high heat and add the onion and thyme. Reduce the heat to medium and cook gently for 20–25 minutes, until the onion starts to caramelise.

Meanwhile, transfer the quail and grapes to the oven and roast for 20 minutes. Toast the bread on both sides in the oven for 12 minutes while the quail are cooking. Rub the toast on one side with the garlic clove.

Remove the quail and grapes from the oven and allow to rest for 10 minutes. Remove the toothpicks.

Meanwhile, add the white wine to the caramelised onion and cook until evaporated, then add the grape juice. Simmer and cook the sauce for 10 minutes, until slightly reduced.

Place a slice of toast, garlic side up, on each plate and spread with ½ tablespoon of the onion jam. Place a quail on top and finish with a little more onion jam. Divide the roasted grapes among the plates and serve immediately.

CONILL AMB XOCOLATA

RABBIT IN CHOCOLATE

Chocolate production in Barcelona is said to date back to the 16th century when Christopher Columbus returned from the Americas with the cocoa bean in his possession. It was initially popularised as a sweet and spicy drink and it wasn't until the 18th century that the chocolate 'bar' was made fashionable by Barcelona's very own Chocolates Amatller, who began to craft truffles and chocolates in different artistic shapes and sizes, including elaborate Easter sculptures and cats' tongues.

Given that it has become custom to eat chocolate rabbits at Easter, perhaps the inspiration came from this traditional Catalan dish, which incorporates chocolate into a savoury offering to enhance the richness and flavour of the rabbit.

Serves 4

2 tablespoons extra virgin olive oil
1 rabbit, cut into 8 pieces (ask
    your butcher to do this for you)
3 tablespoons plain (all-purpose)
    flour
4 shallots, thinly sliced
½ fennel bulb, finely diced, fronds
    reserved for garnish
1 carrot, chopped into 3 cm
    (1¼ in) chunks
½ cinnamon stick
1 sprig rosemary
250 ml (8½ fl oz/1 cup) vi ranci
    or dry sherry
600 ml (20½ fl oz) Brou de
    pollastre (see page 247) or
    store-bought chicken stock
1 teaspoon sea salt
1 teaspoon ground white pepper
100 g (3½ oz) dark chocolate
    (at least 60% cocoa solids),
    chopped
60 ml (2 fl oz/¼ cup) tawny port
    or Pedro Ximénez
2 tablespoons Picada (see
    page 237)
Trinxat (see page 79) or your
    favourite mashed potato,
    to serve

Heat 1 tablespoon of the oil in a heavy-based or cast-iron pan over medium–high heat. Lightly coat the rabbit in the flour, add to the pan and quickly brown on all sides. Transfer to a plate and set aside.

Add the remaining oil to the pan, along with the shallot, fennel, carrot, cinnamon and rosemary and cook for 3 minutes. Deglaze the pan with the vi ranci or sherry until almost evaporated, then add the stock, salt and pepper. Return the rabbit to the pan and bring to a gentle simmer. Reduce the heat to low and partially cover with a lid, leaving an opening for the steam to escape. Cook for 40 minutes, then stir in the chocolate until evenly melted through. Add the port, taste for seasoning and cook for a further 20 minutes, until thickened. At the end of cooking mix through the picada.

Serve on top of trinxat or your favourite mashed potato, and garnish with the fennel fronds. A green salad on the side goes nicely, too.

PERDIU AMB FARCELLETS DE COL

PARTRIDGE & CABBAGE ROLLS

The red-legged partridge is found throughout Southern Europe, but it's not easy to hunt this mountain-dwelling game bird. This traditional recipe is a splendid medieval regal appreciation of the catch, but it's also very simple to make and well worth it.

In lieu of having access to fresh partridge, you can substitute poussin or even chicken marylands (leg quarters). I like to add sour cream to really bring out the decadence of this classic entrée or buffet hero.

Serves 4

1.2 kg (2 lb 10 oz) partridge (or 2 x 600 g/1 lb 5 oz spatchcock/poussin), cleaned and gutted (ask your butcher to do this for you)
3 tablespoons extra virgin olive oil
3 juniper berries, ground using a mortar and pestle
sea salt and freshly cracked black pepper
3 tablespoons duck or goose fat (or butter)
1 leek, white part only, finely diced
1 brown onion, finely diced
4 garlic cloves, chopped
3 celery stalks, finely chopped
2 carrots
2 fresh bay leaves
3 sprigs thyme
125 ml (4 fl oz/½ cup) dry cooking sherry
½ cinnamon stick
500 ml (17 fl oz/2 cups) Brou de pollastre (see page 247) or store-bought chicken stock
8–12 large green cabbage leaves
boiling water
60 ml (2 fl oz/¼ cup) brandy or cognac
2 tablespoons raisins
2 tablespoons chopped chervil or parsley leaves
sour cream, to serve

Lightly coat the partridge in 1 tablespoon of the olive oil and rub the ground juniper berries into the bird. Season with salt and pepper.

Heat 1 tablespoon of the duck fat in a large heavy-based saucepan over medium–high heat. Add the partridge and brown for 2–3 minutes on each side, until golden. Set aside on a plate.

Add the leek, onion, garlic, celery, whole carrots and herbs to the pan, reduce the heat to medium–low and gently cook, stirring regularly, for 15 minutes, or until the onion is soft and caramelised. Pour in the sherry and allow to evaporate, then add the cinnamon and stock. Return the partridge to the pan and bring up to a gentle simmer. Cover and simmer over low heat for 45 minutes.

Soak the cabbage leaves in a bowl of boiling water with a pinch of salt for 2 minutes, then refresh in iced water. Drain and pat dry.

Remove the partridge and carrots from the sauce and set aside to cool. Pull all the meat away from the bones and set aside in a bowl. Discard the bones. Dice the carrots and add to the bowl.

Add the brandy, raisins and 60 ml (2 fl oz/¼ cup) water to the sauce, season with salt and pepper and continue to simmer for 5 minutes, or until you have a thick, chunky sauce. Remove from the heat and add 3 tablespoons to the partridge meat and carrot. Add the chervil or parsley and combine well.

Place a cabbage leaf on a chopping board and place 2 tablespoons of the partridge mixture in the centre of the leaf. Fold over the side closest to you, then tuck in the sides and roll away from you. Gently squeeze the roll in your hand to remove any excess moisture. Repeat with the remaining filling and cabbage leaves. Preheat the oven to 170°C (340°F) fan-forced.

Heat the remaining olive oil and duck fat in a frying pan and add the cabbage rolls, seam side down. Cook the rolls, turning and rotating them, for 3–4 minutes each side, until golden brown all over.

Spoon three-quarters of the sauce into a baking dish and place the cabbage rolls on top. Pour over the remaining sauce and bake for 20 minutes, until the sauce and cabbage rolls are heated through. Serve in the baking dish for everyone to help themselves and with a dollop of sour cream on the side.

CALDERETA
DE XAI

SHEPHERD'S
STEW

This dish encapsulates the flavours of the Catalan mountains, where free-range sheep graze on wild native herbs, such as thyme, rosemary and oregano. I like to add a little ground coriander and fennel seed as well, to add even more floral mountain notes and bring it back to the taste of the local lamb from La Garrotxa county hillsides.

Serves 4

3 tablespoons extra virgin olive oil
3 garlic cloves, skin on, smashed
1 kg (2 lb 3 oz) lamb neck chops, cut in half, leaving the bones attached to one half
sea salt and freshly cracked black pepper
1½ brown onions, finely diced
1 large carrot, finely diced
1 fresh bay leaf
2 sprigs thyme
3 sprigs oregano or marjoram
1 sprig rosemary
1 teaspoon sweet pimentón
1 teaspoon ground coriander seeds
1 teaspoon ground fennel seeds
½ teaspoon ground white pepper
3 medium tomatoes, halved
1 tablespoon tomato paste (concentrated purée)
60 ml (2 fl oz/¼ cup) brandy or cognac
1 litre (34 fl oz/4 cups) Fons fosc de carn (see page 248) or use store-bought beef or veal stock
1 x 400 g (14 oz) tin white beans, such as cannellini (lima), haricot (navy) or great northern, rinsed and drained
crusty baguette, to serve

Heat a large heavy-based stockpot with half the oil and the garlic over medium–high heat. Season the lamb with salt and pepper, add to the pan and sear on both sides until golden. Reduce the heat to medium–low, add the remaining oil, the onion, carrot, herbs, spices, white pepper and 1 teaspoon of salt and sauté for 10 minutes, until the vegetables are soft and starting to colour.

Grate the tomatoes using a coarse grater and discard the skin. Add the tomato and tomato paste to the pot, stir well and cook for 2 minutes, then add the brandy and stock. Cook, with the lid ajar, for 40 minutes, then add the beans. Increase the temperature to high and cook at a rapid simmer, uncovered, for a further 20 minutes to reduce the liquid.

Serve with a crusty baguette on the side.

LLOM AMB LLET I MONGETES

PORK LOIN MEDALLIONS IN MILK WITH WHITE BEANS

'Mongetes' (little nuns) beans are an everyday staple, which are revered in Catalunya, and there are various rural community groups that strive to preserve their heirloom existence. The ganxet is a kidney-shaped white bean grown in Maresme and can be purchased dried, tinned or already cooked in Catalan speciality legume shops.

This dish requires a gentle hand, as you don't want the milk to curdle. The almonds help to prevent this, but you will inevitably notice some of the impurities rising and separating to the top. My chef-trained instincts are always to 'skim the scum', but think of this as an off-white or ivory, still-life Renaissance farmhouse dish and resist the temptation. Thankfully, blending it at the end brings everything happily back together in this winter-warming classic.

Serves 4

800 g–1 kg (1 lb 12 oz–2 lb 3 oz) pork loin medallion, cut into 8 steaks

sea salt and ground white pepper

80 ml (2½ fl oz/⅓ cup) extra virgin olive oil

2 garlic cloves, halved

1 fresh bay leaf

10 black or white peppercorns

¼ nutmeg, freshly grated

40 g (1½ oz/¼ cup) blanched almonds

1 litre (34 fl oz/4 cups) full-cream (whole) milk

250 g (9 oz) dried white beans, such as mongetes or ganxet, soaked overnight (or 1 x 400 g/14 oz tin white beans, rinsed and drained)

1 sprig rosemary plus 1 teaspoon finely chopped rosemary leaves

salt flakes and freshly cracked black pepper

2 red or white witlof (Belgian endive/chicory), halved lengthways

½ teaspoon pink peppercorns

Season the pork steaks with sea salt and white pepper.

Heat half the olive oil in a large frying pan or heavy-based saucepan over high heat. Working in batches, add the steaks and seal for 2–3 minutes on each side. Transfer the steaks to a plate and strain off any excess oil in the pan.

Reduce the heat to medium–high and add the garlic, bay leaf, whole peppercorns, nutmeg and almonds to the pan. Stir and cook until the almonds start to toast and the garlic begins to brown. Pour in the milk and bring to a gentle simmer for 20 minutes. Remove from the heat, discard the bay leaf and blitz the sauce using a hand-held blender until smooth. Add the steaks to the blended milk and simmer over low heat for a further 20 minutes.

Meanwhile, drain the beans and place in a large saucepan with the rosemary sprig. Cover with cold water and bring to the boil. Reduce the heat and simmer for 35–40 minutes, until tender, then drain and place the beans in a medium bowl. Remove and discard the rosemary sprig and add 1 tablespoon of the olive oil, the chopped rosemary and plenty of salt and pepper. Combine well. If using tinned beans, rinse and drain and combine in a bowl with the oil, chopped rosemary and seasoning.

Coat the witlof in the remaining olive oil and chargrill or pan-fry over high heat for 2 minutes on each side to slightly colour.

Serve the pork loins in their sauce with the white beans and grilled witlof on the side and with the pink peppercorns sprinkled over the top.

POLLASTRE
I ESCAMARLANS

CHICKEN & SCAMPI

This is the epitome of 'mar i muntanya' (sea and mountain) and this dish is often simply called just that. The 'pota brava' breed of Catalan chickens, with their blue feet, roam freely around the Llobregat River under the Barcelona airport flight path, and have survived to this day without being crossbred. Certified with a generic denomination, they are the only geographically protected chicken on the Iberian Peninsula that's regulated by the EU. Their meat is very flavoursome with barely any fat, making it a sought-after bird, especially at Christmas, when demand always outnumbers supply.

Scampi are another special local delight and can be found north of Barcelona along the Costa Brava, where ecological aquaculture farms breed amazing-quality seafood.

Serves 4

1.4–1.6 kg (3 lb 1 oz–3½ lb) whole free-range or organic chicken
50 g (1¾ oz/⅓ cup) plain (all-purpose) flour
sea salt and freshly cracked black pepper
3 tablespoons extra virgin olive oil
8 raw scampi or large green prawns (shrimp)
1 red capsicum (bell pepper), thinly sliced
1 brown onion, finely diced
2 garlic cloves, finely chopped
60 ml (2 fl oz/¼ cup) brandy
250 ml (8½ fl oz/1 cup) passata (puréed tomatoes)
1 litre (34 fl oz/4 cups) Brou de pollastre (see page 247) or store-bought chicken stock
3 tablespoons Picada (see page 237)
Patates de pobre (see page 74), to serve

Joint the chicken into eight pieces or ask your butcher to do this for you.

Flour and season the chicken and dust off any excess.

Heat 2 tablespoons of the olive oil in a large frying pan over medium–high heat and, working in batches if necessary, brown the chicken for 4 minutes on all sides until golden. Set aside on a plate. Add the scampi to the pan and cook for 3–4 minutes, until cooked through. Set aside with the chicken.

Reduce the heat to medium, add the remaining olive oil, the capsicum and onion to the pan and cook, stirring frequently, for 8 minutes, until starting to brown. Add the garlic and continue to cook for 4 minutes, then add the brandy and passata and cook for 8–10 minutes, until the sauce has reduced by one-third. Stir through half the chicken stock, then return the chicken to the pan, along with the remaining stock. Simmer for 30–40 minutes, until the sauce has reduced and the chicken is cooked through, then add the picada and keep cooking for a further 10 minutes, adding the scampi back to the pan in the last 2 minutes of cooking.

Serve with patates de pobre.

GALTES DE PORC

BRAISED PORK CHEEKS

This is an inexpensive cut of the pig to try, but you want to get the cheek with the jowl still attached as this is where all the flavour is. This is a deep, hearty, rich, sticky and gelatinous dish that's best cooked as a braise. It's also great to put in a slow cooker in the morning and forget about it for the rest of the day.

As autumn turns into winter, it's very traditional to find this dish on local restaurant menus to coincide with the Catalan season for butchering and making sausages. The orange flavour of the fresh 'picada' goes fantastically with the pork – just like an Italian gremolata served with osso bucco.

Serves 4

80 ml (2½ fl oz/⅓ cup) extra virgin olive oil

4 x 300 g (10½ oz) pork cheeks, jowls attached

1 garlic bulb, cut in half crossways

1 large leek, white part only, finely chopped

120 g (4½ oz) smoky bacon rashers (slices) , finely diced

4 sprigs thyme

2 tablespoons tomato paste (concentrated purée)

4–6 vine-ripened tomatoes, larger ones halved

750 ml (25½ fl oz/3 cups) dry red wine

6–8 parsnips, larger ones halved

½ teaspoon ground cinnamon

sea salt and freshly cracked black pepper

1 orange, zested and halved

6–8 cipollini, shallots or small pickling onions, peeled

1 litre (34 fl oz/4 cups) Forn fosc de carn (see page 248) or store-bought beef stock

40 g (1½ oz/¼ cup) blanched almonds, toasted (or Amettles marconas, see page 18), finely chopped

small handful chopped parsley leaves

crusty bread, to serve

Preheat the oven to 180°C (350°F) fan-forced.

Heat 2 tablespoons of the olive oil in a large flameproof casserole dish over high heat and sear the pork cheeks for 6 minutes on each side until golden. Remove from the dish and set aside.

Add the garlic, leek, bacon and thyme to the dish, reduce the heat to medium and cook for 12–15 minutes, until softened and starting to colour. Add the tomato paste and tomatoes and cook for 4 minutes, stirring continuously, to avoid burning. Pour in half the wine and simmer for 30 minutes, or until reduced by half.

Meanwhile, line a roasting tin with baking paper. Place the parsnips in the tin and toss with 1 tablespoon of the remaining oil, the cinnamon and some salt and pepper, to season.

Return the cheeks to the pan and add the remaining wine, then squeeze over the orange halves and add the cipollini and stock. Season with salt and pepper, then transfer to the middle rack of the oven and roast for 30 minutes.

Pop the parsnips in the oven and turn the cheeks over if they're not completely submerged in the liquid. Roast for a further 30 minutes.

Make a fresh 'picada' by combining the almonds, parsley, orange zest and remaining oil in a small bowl. Season with salt and pepper, to taste.

Divide the cheeks among plates and serve with plenty of sauce, onions and tomatoes. Drizzle the picada over the top and serve with the roasted parsnips and crusty bread on the side.

ESCUDELLA
I CARN D'OLLA

CHRISTMAS SOUP & STEW

There are two parts to this 14th century Christmas ritual followed by a third on San Esteban (Boxing Day) (see page 158), and this magical trio of comfort dishes fills Catalan homes with nostalgia and joy.

The big pot of Catalan 'cocido' (stew) is served up separately as a pasta soup broth for entrée and a large platter of all the poached goodness for mains. This makes a considerable meal, so there will be enough leftovers to make Canelons (see page 158) the following day.

Serves 4

1 pig's trotter
400 g (14 oz) veal shin, rinsed
400 g (14 oz) ham bone, rinsed
200 g (7 oz) dried chickpeas (garbanzo beans) soaked in cold water overnight
2 carrots, halved lengthways
½ green cabbage, halved
2 turnips or parsnips, halved
4 celery stalks, halved
2 leeks, white part only, chopped
250 g (9 oz) pork belly, sliced into 4 pieces
300 g (10½ oz) pork fillet, trimmed and sliced into 4 pieces
1 large black pudding, cut into 4 pieces
2 chicken sausages, halved
500 g (1 lb 2 oz) conchiglie pasta

Pilota

2 chicken livers, trimmed and soaked in milk for 20 minutes
300 g (10½ oz) lean minced (ground) beef
200 g (7 oz) minced (ground) pork
3 garlic cloves, grated
2 tablespoons chopped parsley leaves (stalks finely chopped)
½ teaspoon ground cinnamon
2 tablespoons breadcrumbs
1 egg
sea salt and freshly cracked black pepper
35 g (1¼ oz/¼ cup) plain (all-purpose) flour
½ teaspoon ground white pepper

Place the trotter, veal shin and ham bone in a large stockpot and cover with 6–7 litres (6½–7½ qts) cold water. Set over medium high–heat and bring to a simmer, then reduce the heat to medium–low and let it gently bubble away for about 1 hour, skimming off any impurities that rise to the surface.

Meanwhile, prepare the pilota. Drain and rinse the chicken livers and finely chop, then place in a large bowl with the minced meats, garlic, parsley stalks, cinnamon, breadcrumbs and egg. Season well with salt and pepper and mix to combine. Halve the mixture and shape one half into a large oval football. Combine the flour and white pepper in a bowl and lightly dust the large meatball. Roll the remaining mince into little marbles, dust with the flour and set aside in the fridge.

Drain and rinse the chickpeas and add to the stockpot, along with the giant meatball, vegetables, pork belly and pork fillet. Cook for 30–40 minutes, continuing to skim the surface of the stock as it simmers. Add the black pudding and chicken sausage and cook for a further 30 minutes.

When the chickpeas are soft, ladle three-quarters of the stock into a separate saucepan. Set aside the poached meat and vegetable stew and keep warm, covered with a clean tea towel so it can breathe.

Bring the stock to the boil, add the pasta shells and tiny meatballs and cook for 8–10 minutes, depending on their size.

Ladle the pasta and meatball soup into bowls and sprinkle over the parsley leaves. Serve as an entrée.

After the entrée, quickly bring the poached meat and vegetables to the boil for 5 minutes, or until warmed through. Strain and plate up the meat and vegetables on a large feasting platter with a few spoonfuls of stock poured over to keep them from drying out.

Take it slowly, there's a lot to get through!

CANELONS

BOXING DAY CANNELLONI

A big favourite around Christmas time, this beloved signature Catalan dish is whipped up using all the left-over poached delights from the Christmas Escudella (see page 154). Canelons is also very much a part of everyday life and it is eaten with an almost childish delight throughout the year. It became popular in the 1920s when the bourgeoisie would eat out at trendy restaurants run by northern Italian immigrants, giving this dish a fancy reputation. Thanks to the commercialisation of pasta in the 1950s, it became a lot easier to make, but it's still seen today as a bit of a treat and a specialty, often requested for birthdays and anniversaries.

Serves 4

2 tablespoons extra virgin olive oil
2 brown onions, finely diced
pinch of sea salt
2 garlic cloves, finely chopped
80 ml (2½ fl oz/⅓ cup) dry sherry
   or dry white wine
80 ml (2½ fl oz/⅓ cup) left-over
   Escudella broth (see page 154),
   Brou de pollastre (see page 247)
   or store-bought chicken stock
1 kg (2 lb 3 oz) left-over Escudella
   poached meats (see page 154)
18 cannelloni tubes or fresh
   pasta sheets
freshly cracked black pepper
crusty bread, to serve
green salad leaves, to serve

Béchamel

1 litre (34 fl oz/4 cups) full-cream
   (whole) milk
1 fresh bay leaf
60 g (2 oz) butter, chopped
60 g (2 oz) plain (all-purpose) flour
50 g (1¾ oz) coarsely grated
   pecorino
¼ teaspoon freshly ground
   nutmeg
sea salt and ground white pepper

Heat the olive oil, onion and salt in a medium frying pan over medium–high heat. Cook, stirring frequently, for 10 minutes until soft and starting to colour. Reduce the heat to medium–low, add the garlic and cook for a further 6 minutes. Add the sherry and stir through until completely evaporated, then add the broth. Bring to a simmer and remove from the heat.

Blitz the left-over poached meats in a blender, pulsing several times until evenly chopped. Add the onion and broth mixture and blend to combine into a large meatball-like mass. Add 1 tablespoon water if the mixture is too dry.

To make the béchamel, heat the milk and bay leaf in a medium saucepan over medium heat until steaming and just about to simmer.

In another saucepan, make a roux by melting the butter over medium–low heat, add the flour and cook, stirring with a wooden spoon, until it starts to sizzle and takes on the texture of wet sand.

Remove the bay leaf from the milk, then slowly pour the milk into the roux, stirring constantly to avoid lumps. Simmer for 6–8 minutes, until the sauce thickens, then stir in half the pecorino until melted through. Season with the nutmeg and salt and white pepper.

Preheat the oven to 200°C (400°F) fan-forced.

Stuff the meat mixture into the cannelloni tubes or place 1 heaped tablespoon of the mixture at one end of a pasta sheet and roll up, sealing the seam with a dab of water.

Pour enough béchamel to cover the base of a 30–32 cm (12–12¾ in) long baking dish and place the cannelloni, seam side down, in the dish in a single layer. Cover with the remaining béchamel and sprinkle the remaining pecorino over the top, along with some freshly cracked black pepper.

Bake for 30–40 minutes, until the pasta is cooked through, then blast under a hot grill (broiler) for 6–8 minutes, until the top is golden brown.

Serve with some crusty bread and green salad leaves on the side.

BARNA
MODERNA

MODERN
BARCELONA

Catalunya's beloved capital city, Barcelona, sits on the coast surrounded by mountains, and is an eclectic mix of cosmopolitan tradition, varied history and progressive customs. You can stand at the foot of the Christopher Colombus monument at the base of Les Rambles, stare out to the Mediterranean Sea, then turn 180 degrees and see the mountain of Tibidabo looming over the city, serving as protector and safeguard of the city's people, heritage, architecture and landscape.

Although deeply rooted in Catalan identity, tradition and history, Barcelona is at the same time committed to exploring and incorporating culinary influences from around the world, and has a real desire to evolve and innovate. You only have to visit La Boqueria market in the Ciutat Vella district to see a diverse, culinary melting pot of global ingredients for sale, bought by locals and taken home to be turned into Moroccan, Japanese or perhaps Latin American dishes for an easy weeknight meal.

The New Wave experimental movement in Catalunya has changed the culinary arts from what was a predominantly French school of thinking and technique to a more sharing, curious, experimental, playful and broadminded approach to food and cooking. There are many great Barcelona restaurants creating dishes that display these philosophies: pastries from Pastisseria Escribà or paella from their beach shack Xiringuito Escribà, the ad hoc 'pica pica' plates at Quimet i Quimet, or the more traditional settings of Cal Pep in El Born.

And, of course, it's not only in central Barcelona that you will find this attitude to food. Outside of the city, Catalunya has one of the biggest concentrations of Michelin-starred chefs in the world: Ferran Adrià, Carme Ruscalleda, the Roca brothers and Santi Santamaria in his day. These pioneers have taken the local gastronomy of Catalunya and turned it into something special, where tradition and innovation collide. These dishes are not only some of the most exciting on the global food scene today, they have also been lovingly adopted into the homes of everyday Catalans.

EL BIKINI

HAM & CHEESE TOASTIE

Introduced by the dance club Sala Bikini in the 1950s, which is located in the Les Corts district that's also home to the Camp Nou football stadium, 'el bikini's' popularity as a late night/early morning snack after clubbing is famously Catalan. You'll find them in every bar, especially around universities and schools, where it is the ultimate student morning tea, lunch or afternoon snack.

You can elevate its status by replacing the ham off the bone with jamón ibérico and using manchego cheese or even shaved truffle, but the way I remember it was inhaling a crispy, thin, sweet, white-breaded, salty toastie in three or four bites in the early morning in Bar Estudiantil on Plaça de la Universitat, after a night of dancing at local club La Paloma to sign off the night as complete.

Makes 2 toasties

4 slices high-top sandwich bread, any quality or grain you like

2 tablespoons butter, softened

4 thin slices sweet ham off the bone, such as champagne or Grandmother's ham

4 thin slices havarti (or similar semi-soft, mild white cow's cheese, such as asiago or muenster)

Heat a sandwich press to medium or a large frying pan over medium heat.

Spread the bread with a layer of butter. Place two of the buttered pieces on top of the other slices of bread with the butter facing inwards. Spread the top slices with a little more butter. Place the ham on top, followed by the cheese, then pull the bottom piece of bread out from underneath and close the sandwich, butter side down. Butter the final sides of the bread and toast in the sandwich press or frying pan, making sure each side is golden and crispy and the cheese has melted. Keep the temperature at a medium heat – if it's too low you'll lose all your cheese and if it's too high you'll burn the bread.

Cut in half diagonally and serve with a couple of paper napkins.

SºPA FREDA DE MELÓ

MELON SOUP

The Mediterranean culinary tradition of combining fresh fruit with cured meats lives on strong in this dish. In Catalunya it has transitioned itself into a cold soup, where it is a popular wedding menu entrée at many Barcelona hotels.

You can make this recipe using rockmelon (cantaloupe), watermelon – even kiwi fruit works well – but I've opted for honeydew melon here. Be liberal when peeling to make sure you remove all the bitter pith.

Serves 4

1 kg (2 lb 3 oz) honeydew melon (about 1½ melons), thickly peeled, seeds removed
zest of ½ lime
juice of 1 lime
salt flakes and ground white pepper
8 thin slices jamón
1 bunch mint, leaves picked, reserving a few to garnish
60 ml (2 fl oz/¼ cup) light-tasting extra virgin olive oil

Preheat the oven to 180°C (350°F) fan-forced. Line a baking tray with baking paper.

Slice a thin wedge off the melon and cut the flesh into small dice. Set aside. Blend the remaining melon in a food processor with the lime zest and juice and salt and white pepper, to taste. Add 125 ml (4 fl oz/½ cup) water and blend until smooth. Pour into a large jug and refrigerate.

Lay the jamón on the prepared tray and bake for 12–15 minutes, until crisp.

Bring a small saucepan of water to the boil and blanch the mint leaves for 1 minute. Drain and refresh in iced water, then strain and squeeze out as much water as possible. Transfer the mint to a food processor, add the oil and blend on high until smooth.

Give the melon soup a good stir, then pour into serving bowls. Decorate with the jamón shards and diced melon, drizzle with the infused mint oil and garnish with mint leaves.

ARRÒS CUBÀ

CUBAN RICE

This dish is the go-to hangover lunch when it's too much to bear cooking the ritual Sunday paella. It has made its way into the domestic kitchens of every 'barri' (neighbourhood) surrounding Barcelona, with versions unique to every household. Its variations and success come from the fact that it's a combination of ingredients everyone has lying around their pantries, so when the shops are shut for 'migdiada' (siesta) or on Sundays and you need a quick, tasty meal, this guy is your saviour.

The 'tomàquet fregit' is a supermarket product that Catalans have in their cupboards, and many households cook exclusively with this fried tomato sauce, but I've included a quick homemade version here.

Don't be put off by the unusual mix of ingredients in this dish, it really is the perfect mix of sweet and salty to cure even the most brutal of hangovers.

Serves 4

2 tablespoons extra virgin olive oil
2 garlic cloves, smashed
1 fresh bay leaf
450 g (1 lb) short-grain rice, such as bomba or calasparra, rinsed and drained
pinch of sea salt
4 eggs
2 bananas, halved lengthways
1 teaspoon dried oregano
salt flakes and freshly cracked black pepper

Tomàquet fregit
80 ml (2½ fl oz/⅓ cup) extra virgin olive oil
1½ tablespoons tomato paste (concentrated purée)
2 x 400 g (14 oz) tins chopped tomatoes
¼ teaspoon salt
¼ teaspoon sugar

To make the tomàquet fregit, heat the olive oil in a medium saucepan over medium heat, add the tomato paste and stir through the oil for 4–6 minutes, until beginning to colour. Add the chopped tomatoes, salt and sugar and stir through until starting to bubble. Reduce the heat to low and gently simmer for 20 minutes. Remove from the heat and blitz using a hand-held blender. Set aside in the saucepan and keep warm.

Heat ½ tablespoon of the olive oil in a medium saucepan over medium–high heat, add the garlic and bay leaf and stir through until starting to sizzle. Stir the rice into the pan, add the salt and pour in 950 ml (32 fl oz) water. Cover and bring to the boil, then reduce the heat immediately to medium–low and gently simmer for 8–10 minutes, until nearly all the water has been absorbed. Turn off the heat and let the rice stand for 5 minutes.

Meanwhile, heat the remaining oil in a frying pan over medium heat and fry the eggs and banana.

Spoon the rice into shallow bowls and top with a big ladle of tomàquet fregit. Add the banana and egg and sprinkle with dried oregano, salt flakes and freshly cracked black pepper.

Consume immediately.

MOLLS GAUDÍ

GAUDÍ RED MULLET

This dish evokes the artistic style of architect and innovator Antoni Gaudí's broken ceramic tile mosaics. Its inspiration is a romantic nod to another important Catalan craftsman, the great chef Ferran Adrià, who has also made an innovative, modernist, ground-breaking career by using influences from nature, new techniques and history to produce enchanting and decorative creations. This dish first appeared in 1987 (also the era of the 'mullet' hairdo!) in Adrià's first cookbook *El Bulli: el sabor del Mediterràneo*, and it went on to make regular appearances on his menu at El Bulli until the restaurant closed 25 years later.

This version doesn't involve the molecular gastronomy applied to the original, but the visual senses and common connection between these two great contributors to Catalan culture are colourfully present for all to see.

Serves 4

4 x 100 g (3½ oz) red mullet or pink snapper fillets, skin on, pin-boned

1½ tablespoons extra virgin olive oil

⅓ red capsicum (bell pepper), finely diced

⅓ yellow capsicum (bell pepper), finely diced

1 small zucchini (courgette), finely diced

½ white onion, finely diced

1 tomato, finely diced

⅓ bunch chives, finely chopped

salt flakes and freshly cracked black pepper

oil spray

Preheat a grill (broiler) to medium–high. Cut out four squares of baking paper just larger than the fish fillets.

Brush the fish skin with a little of the olive oil and place each fillet on the prepared baking paper.

Combine the capsicums, zucchini, onion, tomato and chives in a small bowl and season to taste. Evenly flatten the mixture onto the oiled fish skin.

Heat the remaining oil in a medium non-stick frying pan over high heat and gently slide each fillet off the paper into the pan, decorated side up. Cook for 2 minutes to seal the base of the fish, then carefully transfer the fish back onto the baking paper squares and grill (broil) for 4–6 minutes, until lightly toasted.

Serve with a sauce if you like – Alberginia i nous (see page 234), Salsa almadroc (see page 235) or Salsa romesco (see page 236) would all work well, but this dish is equally decadent on its own as a delicate entrée or as a substantial main with your favourite salad.

PURÉ DE MONGETES I BOTIFARRA NEGRA

WHITE BEAN PURÉE & BOTIFARRA

This is a popular canapé that's often served at functions. Barcelona's trade fair institution, Fira de Barcelona, in Monjuic, holds a lot of international events, festivals and conferences, and this was a favourite combination of mine that we used to serve at the VIP tents when I worked there in the central kitchen. It's sweet and earthy and gritty, just like life in Barcelona!

Makes 12

6 garlic cloves, halved
375 ml (12½ fl oz/1½ cups) full-cream (whole) milk
400 g (14 oz) tin cannellini (lima) beans, rinsed and drained
2 tablespoons blanched almonds, toasted
salt flakes and ground white pepper
2 black puddings, de-cased
1 medium baguette, cut into 12 slices
60 ml (2 fl oz/¼ cup) light-tasting extra virgin olive oil, plus extra if necessary
½ teaspoon vanilla bean paste
micro sorrel leaves, to garnish

Place the garlic and milk in a small saucepan over medium heat and gently simmer for 10 minutes, until the garlic is soft.

Strain the garlic and transfer to a food processor, along with the white beans and almonds, and blitz until smooth. Add a little of the blanching milk if the mixture is too thick to blend in your machine and blend again. Season to taste with salt and white pepper.

Fry the black pudding mince in a small frying pan over medium–high heat, stirring and breaking up any larger pieces with a wooden spoon, until the fat has rendered and the meat starts to crisp and resemble crumbs. Remove the mince from the pan, then reduce the heat and fry the baguette slices (in batches if necessary) on both sides, until toasted. Add a little oil if the pan is drying out.

Mix the olive oil and vanilla bean paste in a small bowl.

Line up the toast on a serving tray and spread the white bean purée on the toast. Sprinkle over the black pudding crumbs, drizzle with the vanilla oil and garnish with micro sorrel leaves.

SALMÓ CONFITAT

CONFIT SALMON

The Catalans are confit kings. Instead of the house-made gravlax you usually see on restaurant menus, in Barcelona it will be a confit salmon, tuna or bacalllà (salt cod) salad. It's especially popular around the Ciutat Vella, Barri Gòtic and El Born neighbourhoods, feeding the hordes of hungry tourists who wander through.

This is a delicate, gentle way to cook fish without compromising texture or flavour. You can also confit larger-sized fillets for a longer time and flake the fish through a simple green leaf salad with the green beans.

Serves 4

600 g (1 lb 5 oz) fresh salmon fillet, skin removed, pin-boned and cut into 2 cm (¾ in) cubes
500 ml (17 fl oz/2 cups) light-tasting extra virgin olive oil
6 juniper berries, bruised or smashed open slightly
1 lemon, peeled and cut into segments, peel reserved
2 sprigs thyme
200 g (7 oz) green beans, trimmed
½ bunch dill, finely chopped
1 tablespoon sherry vinegar
pinch of salt flakes
1 frisée (curly endive), inner leaves only
½ white salad onion, thinly sliced
1 tablespoon salmon caviar pearls

Combine the salmon, olive oil, juniper berries, lemon peel and thyme in a heatproof glass or ceramic baking dish and set aside for 2 hours to marinate.

Preheat the oven to its lowest setting, about 60°C (140°F) fan-forced.

Place the fish in the oven and cook for 12 minutes or up to 20 minutes if you prefer your fish well cooked. Remove from the oven and let the salmon cool down in the oil.

Blanch the green beans in salted boiling water for 2 minutes, then drain and plunge into iced water to stop the cooking process. Slice the beans in half lengthways.

Combine the dill with 3 tablespoons of the confit oil, the sherry vinegar and salt flakes in a small bowl.

Strain the confit salmon and discard the oil.

Place the frisée leaves and green beans on a serving platter and arrange the lemon segments, onion and confit salmon over the top. Drizzle with the dill dressing and scatter over the caviar pearls.

CAP I POTA TERRINA

NOSE-TO-TAIL TERRINE

Translated literally as the head and feet of the pork, this dish is not to everyone's taste, but it's a real treat for terrine aficionados, brought back into 'moda' (fashion) by chef Carles Gaig and proudly served up to foreigners as a bit of a national sport to see their reaction!

It was traditionally served as a peasant stew to use up all the bits and bobs left over from the 'matança' (slaughter) that you couldn't make into charcuterie or sausages. This contemporary pressed terrine isn't as intense in flavour as the old, warm, stewed version, instead it's clean and light with a nice nod to tradition.

Serves 8–12

1 x 600 g (1 lb 5 oz) pig's head
2 pigs' trotters
400 g (14 oz/1½ cups) fine sea salt
250 ml (8½ fl oz/1 cup) dry white wine
freshly cracked black pepper
1½ tablespoons white peppercorns
2 onions, halved
2 carrots
3 celery stalks
3 fresh bay leaves
6 sprigs parsley, leaves chopped, stalks reserved
4 sprigs thyme
1 tablespoon sherry or white wine vinegar

To serve
dijon mustard
horseradish cream
cornichons
melba toasts

Soak the head and trotters in 4 litres (4¼ qts) water and the salt overnight. Drain and rinse well.

Place the head and trotters in a large stockpot, cover with water and bring to the boil over high heat. Reduce the heat to a gentle simmer and add the wine, pepper, peppercorns, vegetables, bay leaves, parsley stalks, half the thyme and the vinegar. Simmer for 3–4 hours, until the pig is tender and the jaw bone is falling away from the cheeks.

Remove the meat from the stock and set aside. Strain the stock, discard the solids and return the liquid to the boil and reduce by one-third. Spoon a few tablespoons onto a plate and refrigerate for 10 minutes to test the gelatine. If it sets, the liquid is ready; if not, return to a simmer and reduce further.

Remove the liquid from the heat and set aside until cool enough to touch, then stir through the chopped parsley leaves.

Pick and dice all the meat from the pig and discard the bones, teeth and eyes.

Line a 1.3 litre (44 fl oz) terrine mould with two layers of plastic wrap, fill with the chopped meat and pour the liquid on top. Sit the remaining thyme sprigs on top of the liquid.

Refrigerate overnight and slice the following day. Serve on a wooden board or platter with mustard, horseradish, cornichons and melba toasts, and tuck in as you would a cheese board.

FORMATGE DE CABRA GRATINAT

PAN-FRIED GOAT'S CHEESE SALAD

This simple, go-to warm salad is a modern Barna favourite served in restaurants throughout the city. It's also very popular at functions, where it's often served as an entrée.

The fats in the goat's cheese make it an ideal cheese to fry with as you can get a crusty seal without the milk oils separating. Rinded goat's cheese is a French product and its soft, creamy and acidic flavour pairs perfectly here with the sweet vinaigrette and fresh bitter leaves.

Serves 4

2 tablespoons raisins
60 ml (2 fl oz/¼ cup) balsamic vinegar
1 teaspoon honey
80 ml (2½ fl oz/⅓ cup) extra virgin olive oil
3 tablespoons walnuts, toasted and chopped
½ teaspoon salt flakes
250 g (9 oz) goat's cheese log with rind, cut into 1–2 cm (½–¾ in) thick slices
freshly cracked black pepper
½ radicchio, leaves separated
70 g (2½ oz) rocket (arugula) leaves
1 red apple, cored and thinly sliced
½ bunch chives, cut into 3 cm (1¼ in) lengths

Heat the raisins and balsamic vinegar in a small saucepan over medium heat and simmer for 4–5 minutes to rehydrate the raisins. Stir through the honey and remove from the heat. Allow to cool a little then pour in the olive oil and mix through the walnuts and salt flakes. Keep at room temperature.

Line a baking tray with baking paper.

Heat a large non-stick frying pan over high heat. When the pan is extremely hot, add the cheese and cook for 1–2 minutes each side. Transfer to the prepared tray and crack some black pepper over the top.

Arrange the salad leaves on serving plates and top with the apple and fried goat's cheese.

Spoon over the dressing and rain over the chives.

LA TRUITA DE PATATES XIPS

POTATO CHIP TORTILLA

Ferran Adrià is the gastronimcal leader of Catalan cuisine in the modern era. Yes, there are others but his openness and playful, curious and generous approach to cooking has been embraced the world over and in Catalunya he is truly a national treasure.

Invented by Adrià and interpreted by many, this is one of those unintentionally political dishes that takes the original 'tortilla española' (Spanish tortilla) recipe and dares to simplify and modernise it for the home cook, so that even a teenager can be bothered to attempt it. Removing the 'española' part of the Spanish tortilla, Ferran turned the humble 'truita' into a unique 'hack' version, swerving not too far from the original, yet giving it a new Catalan identity for the sheer fact that he invented it and he is Catalan!

Olé!

I can't do without sweet caramelised onions in my tortilla, though.

Serves 4

1 tablespoon extra virgin olive oil
1½ brown onions, finely diced
¼ teaspoon sea salt
6 large eggs
60 ml (2 fl oz/¼ cup) full-cream (whole) milk
170 g (6 oz) good-quality salted potato chips (crisps)
Pa amb tomàquet (see page 22), to serve

Heat half the olive oil in a small–medium non-stick frying pan over low heat. Add the onion and salt and sweat for 15 minutes, until completely soft and starting to colour. Remove from the heat and allow to cool.

Meanwhile, beat the eggs and milk in a bowl. Tip the potato chips into the egg mixture to soak, completely covering every chip. Let stand for 10 minutes.

Return the pan with the onion to medium heat, add a drizzle more oil and pour in the egg mixture, stirring to help the egg begin to cook evenly. When the egg just starts to scramble, turn the heat to low and flatten the mixture with a spatula, smoothing out the top and around the edge of the pan. Shake the pan slightly and when the bottom of the egg has set, place a large dinner plate over the top and, using a tea towel to grip the frying pan handle, flip the 'truita' over onto the plate. Add the remaining oil to the pan and slide the tortilla back into the pan. Tuck in the sides with the spatula and cook for another 2–3 minutes. Turn off the heat and cover with the dinner plate again while it rests for a few minutes.

Turn out onto a plate and serve with pa amb tomàquet.

TÀRTAR DE TONYINA

TUNA TARTARE

Barcelona has been dishing up the classic steak tartare for as long as any other city, and with the rise in popularity of Asiatic cuisine and a growing focus on health, this dish is a leaner, lighter, modern adjustment to the classic, which is found on menus throughout the city, side by side, of course, its founding father. The addition of truffles and olive oil to this recipe stamps it as a truly cosmopolitan Mediterranean fusion favourite.

Serves 4

2 teaspoons light soy sauce

1 teaspoon sesame oil

½ teaspoon freshly grated ginger

sea salt and freshly cracked
    black pepper

400 g (14 oz) sushi-grade tuna,
    diced into 1 cm (½ in) cubes

2 limes, 1 peeled and roughly
    chopped, 1 juiced

¼ bunch chives, finely chopped

1 avocado, diced

1 teaspoon truffle paste or oil

1 tablespoon olive oil

2 tablespoons black and white
    sesame seeds, toasted

2 teaspoons fried shallots

Combine the soy sauce, sesame oil, ginger and salt and pepper in a bowl to make a dressing. Toss through the tuna and set aside in the fridge.

In another bowl, carefully combine the chopped lime, lime juice, chives and avocado and season with salt and pepper.

Combine the truffle paste and olive oil in a small bowl.

Gently combine the tuna and avocado mixture in a bowl, then spoon onto serving plates, sprinkle with the sesame seeds and fried shallots and drizzle with the truffle oil.

CARPACCIO DE POP

OCTOPUS CARPACCIO

Like the tartare, the carpaccio is another favourite served in Catalan restaurants. Italian in origin and usually a raw offering, this carpaccio is actually cooked then moulded, cooled, thinly sliced and dressed.

Inspired by the famous 'pulpo gallego' (Galician-style octopus) with pimentón, you can double the recipe and use a rectangular terrine mould instead of the inventive recycled, round plastic bottle trick. Just make sure to weight down the top of the terrine while it's setting in the fridge to compact it properly.

Serves 4–6

1 small fennel bulb, quartered
1 carrot, halved
1 onion, quartered
8 garlic cloves, peeled
2 fresh bay leaves
10 peppercorns
2 sprigs thyme
2 star anise
2 tablespoons sea salt
2 tablespoons sherry vinegar
1.2–1.5 kg (2 lb 10 oz–3 lb 5 oz) whole octopus, beak and eyes removed, cleaned and rinsed (alternatively ask your fishmonger to do this for you)
1 teaspoon smoked pimentón
2 tablespoons extra virgin olive oil
sea salt and freshly cracked black pepper
1 lemon
1 tablespoon chopped parsley leaves
1 tablespoon finely chopped chives

In a large stockpot, bring 4 litres (4¼ qts) water, the vegetables, garlic, bay leaves, peppercorns, thyme and star anise to a simmer over medium heat, then stir through the salt. Holding the octopus by the head, dip the tentacles in and out of the hot stock five or six times, until the tentacles start to curl, then lower the whole octopus into the pot. Simmer for 1 hour, then turn off the heat and allow the octopus to cool in the liquid for another 30 minutes to tenderise further. Strain the octopus and set aside to cool. Discard the stock.

Place the octopus on a clean chopping board and cut the head away from the tentacles. Cut the head in half, then divide into quarters, leaving the tentacles intact. Transfer the cut octopus to a bowl and add the pimentón and 2 teaspoons of the olive oil. Season with salt and pepper and mix well.

Take a clean 1 litre (34 fl oz/4 cup) disposable plastic water or soft drink bottle and cut the top one-third off the bottle. Pierce two small holes in the base and cut six slits down from the rim to create tabs.

Stand the bottle inside a bowl and tightly arrange the octopus in the base of the plastic bottle mould, pressing down with a pestle or potato masher to release any air bubbles – you want the octopus to be well compacted. Fold the cut plastic tabs over the top of the octopus and wrap tightly with plastic wrap. Refrigerate for 5–6 hours, until completely set.

Peel the lemon and segment it over a small bowl to catch the juice. Roughly chop the segments and add to the bowl, along with the remaining olive oil, fresh herbs and a little salt and pepper. Whisk to make a dressing.

Remove the octopus from the fridge, unwrap and turn out upside down onto a clean chopping board. Slice as thinly as you can using an electric knife or by hand using a very sharp knife.

Arrange the carpaccio on a large platter or on individual plates. Serve immediately with a drizzle of the dressing or refrigerate until required to keep the circular form set.

POLLASTRE A'LAST

ROTISSERIE CHICKEN

In Catalunya, this dish is a Sunday night summer classic for when it's too hot to cook or too much effort after a weekend at the beach. Every town has a local chicken shop that sells rotisserie chicken, which locals pick up on their way home and serve simply with 'patates'. I was first introduced to this cheap and cheerful meal at the infamous 'Pollo Rico', after bar-hopping late at night in the El Raval neighbourhood.

This is a make-at-home, slow-cooked, smoked barbecue version that you can put on the barbecue in the afternoon and leave while you have a 'siesta', do some gardening or watch the tennis (or Tour de France if in Europe).

Serves 4

1.6 kg (3½ lb) whole free-range chicken, rinsed
3 tablespoons extra virgin olive oil
4 large potatoes, halved
2 teaspoons sea salt
1 teaspoon onion powder
½ teaspoon garlic powder
½ teaspoon smoked pimentón
1 teaspoon dried oregano
½ teaspoon ground white pepper
125 ml (4 fl oz/½ cup) dry white wine
salt flakes
1 x quantity Salsa de julivert (see page 240)
1 x quantity Allioli (see page 244), to serve

Dislocate the chicken hips by placing it breast side down and use your thumbs to push the tops of the thigh joints in on themselves towards the breast and then out away from the chicken frame. Pat the chicken dry inside and out with paper towel, then place in the fridge to air-dry for 2 hours.

Preheat a barbecue or smoker to high (220°C/440°F).

Drizzle 2 tablespoons of the olive oil over the potato halves, sprinkle with half the salt and wrap in foil.

Remove the chicken from the fridge and rub with the remaining olive oil.

Combine the onion and garlic powders, pimentón, oregano, white pepper and remaining salt in a small bowl, then evenly dust all over the chicken.

Place the chicken, breast side up, on a wire rack and sit in a large baking dish. Pour the wine and 500 ml (17 fl oz/2 cups) water into the dish, then transfer to the barbecue, close the lid and cook for 20 minutes, before reducing the heat to low (120°C/240°F). Open the lid, throw the jacket potatoes on the grill plate and turn the chicken over. Close the lid and leave to cook for 1½ hours. Turn the chicken over one more time, pour another 500 ml (17 fl oz/2 cups) water into the base of the dish and cook for a further 1 hour.

Turn the heat off and let the chicken rest inside the barbecue for 20 minutes before carving.

Crack open the potato jackets, sprinkle with salt flakes and serve with your favourite cut of chicken, plenty of salsa julivert and mountains of allioli.

FOIE GRAS AMB
LLENTIES BELUGA

SEARED
FOIE GRAS &
LENTIL SALAD

The bourgeoisie of Barcelona have an obsession with foie gras – perhaps not quite as much as the French, but close. And lentils for that matter, too.

This dish is a classic new-money combination of the rich and the poor, following a long tradition of pairing luxury ingredients with peasant produce to a distinct level of refinement. The crusty, seared, salty foie gras next to the soft, earthy lentils and fresh, crunchy raw vegetables is a winning cocktail of textures and flavours that's hard to beat.

Return this dish to its peasant roots, if you like, and use tinned tuna instead of foie gras, a tin of lentils and whatever veggies you have lying around. I survived on this in my twenties, while saving to travel and living alone in a tiny flat next to the Palau de la Música. I would skip home over Les Rambles after cooking all day at café Kasparo in the Ciutat Vella, and whip up this salad in a flash for dinner.

Serves 4

300 g (10½ oz) beluga lentils, soaked in 2 litres (68 fl oz/ 8 cups) water overnight
1 fresh bay leaf
2 sprigs thyme
1 garlic clove, minced
1½ teaspoons dijon mustard
juice of ½ lemon
1 tablespoon sherry or red wine vinegar
2½ tablespoons extra virgin olive oil
salt flakes and freshly cracked black pepper
1 carrot, finely diced
½ fennel bulb, finely diced
2 celery heart stalks, finely diced, leaves reserved for garnish
½ red onion, finely diced
3 radicchio leaves, roughly torn
2 tablespoons chervil or flat-leaf parsley, chopped
⅓ bunch chives, finely chopped
2 duck foie gras, sliced in half lengthways

Drain and rinse the lentils, then place in a large stockpot with more than enough water to fully cover them over medium heat. Add the bay leaf and thyme and bring to a simmer for 15 minutes, or until just tender but not falling apart. Remove from the heat and transfer the lentils and cooking liquid to a baking dish to cool down a little. If they are really tender, skip this process and drain them straight away. Rinse them under cold water if they are already starting to fall apart. You will compromise flavour but you won't be left with mushy lentils.

In a small bowl, make a dressing with the garlic, mustard, lemon juice, vinegar, 2 tablespoons of the olive oil and salt and pepper, to taste.

Once the lentils have cooled slightly, drain and toss with the dressing while still warm. Set aside to cool completely, then mix through the finely diced vegetables, radicchio and herbs.

Heat the remaining olive oil in a large frying pan over medium–high heat. Sear the foie gras for 1–2 minutes on each side, then remove the pan from the heat and allow the foie gras to stand for another 1–2 minutes. It might be slightly pink still but it will carry on cooking. Transfer to paper towel and season heavily with salt flakes.

Divide the lentils among bowls, top with the foie gras and reserved celery leaves and serve.

MADUIXES AMB PEBRE I BALSÀMIC

STRAWBERRIES WITH PEPPER & BALSAMIC

The wild, forest alpine strawberries 'maduixes del bosc' grown in Catalunya are prized by pastry chefs and speciality fruit suppliers throughout Europe for their prettiness and superior fragrance and flavour. Similar in size and shape to a small raspberry, they make for very decorative arrangements on top of cakes and slices. Here, the humble seasonal field strawberry will do.

A quick and simple but sophisticated combination, you'll find this dessert on menus around Barcelona often served with a vanilla panna cotta, ice cream, almond cream (see page 210) or simply on their own to cleanse the palate after a long lunch.

Serves 4

2 punnets (500 g/1 lb 2 oz) strawberries, hulled, larger ones halved

3 tablespoons pure icing (confectioners') sugar, plus extra to serve

1½ tablespoons aged balsamic vinegar

2 teaspoons black peppercorns, crushed in a mortar and pestle, or to taste

2 teaspoons pink peppercorns

Sprinkle the berries with the icing sugar and balsamic vinegar in a large bowl. Add the black pepper and allow to sit for 10 minutes.

Transfer to a serving bowl, sprinkle with the pink peppercorns and sift over a little extra icing sugar.

MACEDÒNIAN DE FRUITA

MACEDONIAN FRUIT SALAD

Fresh fruit is commonly served for dessert in Catalunya, and while the name obviously indicates this dish is not of Catalan origin, the Macedonian fruit salad is enjoyed throughout Europe, Argentina and other Latin American countries where it is even sold in tins.

Indicative of the ethnic diversity of Alexander the Great's empire, this medley of fruit brings together a wide range of colours, flavours, textures and shapes.

Serves 4

¼ honeydew melon, peeled, seeds removed
¼ watermelon, peeled, seeds removed
seeds of 1 pomegranate
¼ pineapple, peeled, cored and diced
200 g (7 oz) mixed berries
1 kiwi fruit, diced
1 mandarin, segmented
2 figs, quartered
juice of 1 orange
zest and juice of 1 lime
½ tablespoon pure icing (confectioners') sugar
mint leaves, to garnish
edible flowers, to garnish (optional)

Use a melon baller to scoop out balls from the honeydew melon and watermelon. Transfer to a large bowl, add the remaining ingredients and stir well to combine.

Serve in bowls garnished with fresh mint leaves and edible flowers, if using.

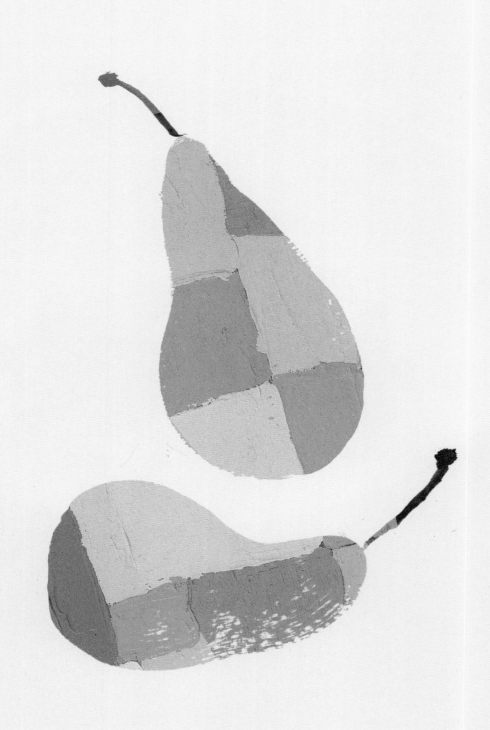

DOLÇOS

SWEETS

As important as 'pica pica' or la comida (lunch), Catalunya's sweet offerings epitomise the gesture and hospitality of family and community. Catalans always have dessert and especially at lunch, where a meal is not complete without a piece of fresh seasonal fruit or yoghurt, or perhaps something more indulgent, such as a pudding, flan, crema or cake.

The history of many Catalan desserts is firmly placed in peasant fare, where the glut of seasonal ingredients was used to create something sweet to end the meal. Nuts, fruits and even vegetables were turned into desserts, with often nothing more than the addition of sugar or honey for sweetness. Sometimes cheese was eaten, but always with a sweet counterpart, such as quince paste (see page 226). Perhaps the most famous Catalan dessert is the Crema catalana (see page 200), Catalunya's answer to the crème brûlée and a classic in its own right. Consisting of just four basic ingredients, it exemplifies how something truly decadent can be made using only the produce in the local surrounding area, plus the addition of a little sugar.

Desserts and cakes are also tied to religious 'festes' (festivals) and holidays, and each occasion is marked by a specific sweet treat to be shared with friends and family. Tradition dictates that you don't pass All Saints' Day on 1 November without eating a 'panellet' (see page 202) after visiting the graves of loved ones past; the Twelfth Day of Christmas is always celebrated with the famous Three Kings' cake (see page 220); while the summer solstice is never complete without a piece of Coca de Sant Joan (see page 223), a yeasted cake sandwiched with a sweet jam filling that's always shared with neighbours, work colleagues, friends and family. It is these traditions and customs that help keep the Catalan culture alive through its relationship with food and ensure that Catalunya's unique culinary heritage will be preserved for generations to come.

CREMA CATALANA

CATALAN CRÈME BRÛLÉE

The French compete with Catalunya for the origin of this famous dish; however, there are some small differences. Quicker, easier and cheaper, the Catalans cook out the egg a little further on the stovetop and set their custards in the fridge with the help of cornflour (cornstarch), as historically many people didn't have access to ovens. They also use milk, not cream – another peasant compromise.

Makes 4–6

1 litre (34 fl oz/4 cups) full-cream (whole) milk
1 cinnamon stick
peel of ½ lemon
peel of ½ orange
7 large egg yolks
200 g (7 oz) caster (superfine) sugar
3 tablespoons cornflour (cornstarch)

Gently warm the milk, cinnamon and citrus peels in a medium saucepan over medium–low heat until just until simmering. Remove from the heat and allow to stand for 15 minutes for the flavours to infuse.

Whisk the egg yolks in a large heatproof bowl, then whisk in 150 g (5½ oz) of the sugar until creamy. Whisk in the cornflour until well combined.

Strain the warmed milk into a jug, then slowly pour into the egg mixture, whisking to combine.

Pour the custard back into a clean saucepan and return to medium–low heat, stirring continuously with a wooden spoon or silicon spatula. Allow to gently simmer and bubble, moving the custard constantly to avoid scrambling on the bottom.

When thick and coating the back of the spoon, remove from the heat and strain through a fine sieve. This will pick up any scrambled egg from the base of the saucepan.

Evenly divide the custard among 4–6 ramekins, leaving a 5 mm (¼ in) gap at the top of each ramekin. Transfer to a tray and allow to cool slightly before refrigerating for at least 4 hours or ideally overnight.

To serve, sprinkle the remaining sugar over the top of the custards and caramelise to a hard crust using a blow torch or sugar iron.

You can also caramelise the set custards under the grill (broiler). Place the custards in a baking dish half-filled with iced water, sprinkle the sugar over the ramekins and grill (broil) until well caramelised.

PANELLETS DE PINYONS

ALL SAINTS' DAY SWEETS

La Castanyada is an ancient festival celebrated the day before All Saints' Day. It coincides with chestnut season in Catalunya and you'll find pop-up stalls around Barcelona roasting chestnuts in big wood-fired metal drums and serving them up in little newspaper cones. It's traditional to eat these after visiting the graves of family members and loved ones on All Saints' Day and then wander into a bakery for some 'panellets'. Unfortunately, nowadays Halloween has crept in to compete with this ancient funeral ritual.

There are several versions of these little balls and they can be flavoured with coconut, coffee, orange, almonds or chestnuts, but it's the pine nuts that are the real star that everyone goes for.

Makes 20

200 g (7 oz) sweet potato, peeled and chopped into large even-sized chunks
300 g (10½ oz) fine almond meal
2 eggs, separated
½ teaspoon almond extract
180 g (6½ oz) icing (confectioners') sugar
zest of ½ lemon
1½ tablespoons extra virgin olive oil
250 g (9 oz) pine nuts

Bring a saucepan of water to the boil and steam or boil the sweet potato for 6–8 minutes, until tender. Transfer to a bowl and mash with the back of a fork. Mix in the almond meal, then add the egg whites and almond extract and mix to combine. Fold through the sugar and lemon zest, then transfer the mixture to a clean work surface. Using slightly wet hands, roll into an even 3–4 cm (1¼–1½ in) thick log. Wrap in baking paper and refrigerate for 1–2 hours to firm up.

Whisk the oil and egg yolks in a small bowl.

Preheat the oven to 170°C (340°F) fan-forced. Line a baking tray with baking paper.

Remove the log from the fridge, cut into 20 even-sized pieces and roll into balls. Place the pine nuts in a medium bowl and roll each ball around, gently pressing to adhere the pine nuts. Set aside on the prepared tray and lightly brush each one with the egg yolk mix.

Bake for 15–20 minutes, until golden. The panellets will keep in an airtight container for 4–5 days.

MEL I MATÓ

HONEY & GOAT'S CURD

'Mató' also known as 'requesòn' simply means curds, and this dish is an ode to the farm. If you are fortunate enough to have access to milk and honey direct from the source, this simple dessert will be even more special. I sometimes add a sprig of thyme or a fresh bay leaf to the milk while heating, especially in winter, to give more depth of flavour. I also like to sprinkle over bee pollen at the end or you could add your favourite toasted nuts.

In some rural taverns, they serve this dish still warm on the plate – it's that fresh.

Serves 4

1 litre (34 fl oz/4 cups) full-cream
    (whole) goat's milk
juice of 1 lemon
100 g (3½ oz) honey
100 g (3½ oz) honeycomb
2 teaspoons bee pollen

Slowly bring the milk to a simmer in a heavy-based saucepan over medium heat. Remove from the heat. Pour the lemon juice into the hot milk and gently move the liquid around until it starts to separate. Set aside for 10 minutes to settle the curds.

Strain the curds into a fine sieve lined with muslin (cheesecloth), then set aside for 1–2 hours or place in the fridge for 4 hours if you prefer a firmer 'mató'.

Divide among bowls, spoon over the honey and honeycomb and sprinkle with the pollen.

POSTRES DE MÚSIC

MUSICIAN'S DESSERT

This dish is very Catalan. It's traditionally what musicians took with them after lunch, carried in their pockets to keep them going while they played in village celebrations, missing out on the daily 'siesta'. You can use any combination of your favourite fruit and nuts and either serve them all mixed up in a bowl or arrange each component neatly on a plate.

I've included a recipe here for candied walnuts (nous garrapinyats), which are often served hot in cones at markets and fairs.

This dessert should always be accompanied by a glass of Moscatel, or your favourite sticky wine or sweet sherry.

Serves 4

40 g (1½ oz/¼ cup) raw almonds, toasted
35 g (1¼ oz/¼ cup) hazelnuts, roasted, skins rubbed off
3 tablespoons pine nuts, toasted
8 dried apricots
4 dried pear halves
large handful golden raisins or dried muscatel grapes

Brandy figs

8 whole dried figs
60 ml (2 fl oz/¼ cup) brandy
1 tablespoon boiling water
2 tablespoons honey

Candied walnuts

300 g (10½ oz) whole walnuts
300 g (10½ oz) caster (superfine) sugar

Optional additions

large handful chocolate-covered scorched almonds
fresh figs or grapes
any other dried fruit, such as papaya, mango, dates or prunes

To make the brandy figs, soak the figs in the brandy and boiling water for a minimum of 2 hours. Remove the figs and place the brandy liquid in a small bowl. Stir through the honey.

Preheat the oven to 140°C (275°F) fan-forced. Line a baking tray with baking paper.

To make the candied walnuts, spread the walnuts out on the prepared tray and bake for 8–10 minutes. Remove from the oven and set aside.

Meanwhile, combine the sugar and 60 ml (2 fl oz/¼ cup) water in a small saucepan over medium–low heat and simmer, without stirring, until lightly golden. Add the walnuts and quickly stir to coat them in the syrup, then spread out on the lined baking tray and set aside to cool.

Arrange all the ingredients on a platter and drizzle with the brandy–honey syrup. Serve in the centre of the table with your favourite Spanish tipple.

MENJAR BLANC

ALMOND CREAM

This dessert is a familiar face in many countries in Europe. Literally translated as 'white food' it has versions in Turkish, French and British cuisines. Even the Italian panna cotta is not far removed.

Dating back to the 14th century, the recipe first appeared in the Valencian cookbook, *Libre de Sent Soví,* published in 1324, one of the oldest cookbooks in Europe. There is some evidence that 'menjar blanc' was originally an Arab dish brought back by the Crusaders. The monks of Reus and Tarragona would make this pudding during Lent when no animal products were permitted, but today it's a staple Catalan dessert made all year round.

I love serving this with fresh cherries when they're in season.

Serves 4–6

peel of 1 lemon
1 cinnamon stick
½ vanilla bean, split and seeds scraped
500 g (1 lb 2 oz) blanched almonds
150 g (5½ oz) icing (confectioners') sugar
100 g (3½ oz) rice flour
2 drops almond extract
ground cinnamon, to serve
biscotti, to serve

Place the lemon peel, cinnamon, vanilla bean and seeds and 500 ml (17 fl oz/2 cups) water in a medium saucepan. Bring to a rolling boil, add the almonds and bring back to the boil for 2 minutes. Remove from the heat and allow to stand for 10 minutes. Scoop out the cinnamon stick, lemon peel and vanilla bean and blend the almonds and the liquid to a paste using a hand-held blender. Strain through a fine sieve lined with muslin (cheesecloth) into a bowl, squeezing out as much liquid as possible from the almond pulp. You should have about 700 ml (23½ fl oz) of liquid.

Bring 1 litre (34 fl oz/4 cups) water to the boil in another saucepan, then remove from the heat and add all the almond pulp. Stir to combine, then strain again into the almond milk in the bowl. You should have about 1 litre (34 fl oz/4 cups) of liquid. Discard the pulp.

Pour the almond milk into a saucepan over medium heat and add the sugar. Gently heat until the milk starts to steam and the sugar has completely dissolved. Remove from the heat.

Make a slurry with the rice flour and 200 ml (7 fl oz) water and pour into the heated milk. Stir through the almond extract, then divide among 4–6 pudding bowls and set aside in the fridge to completely chill for 4 hours.

Sprinkle a little ground cinnamon over each pudding and serve with biscotti.

FARINETES DE FAJOL

BUCKWHEAT CAKE

This sweet treat is typically found in the region of La Garrotxa where the main source of food for the local goats is the green crop of buckwheat, which results in a nutty, herbaceous-tasting 'Garrotxa' semi-firm goat's cheese.

This super-simple peasant dish is essentially a set porridge that's sliced, fried and then sugared to eat!

Makes 10–12 slices

1 tablespoon extra virgin olive oil, plus extra for greasing
pinch of salt
125 g (4½ oz) buckwheat flour
250 ml (8½ fl oz/1 cup) light-tasting olive oil
250 g (9 oz) caster (superfine) sugar

Lightly grease a 20 cm x 10 cm (8 in x 4 in) loaf (bar) tin.

Heat the extra virgin olive oil, salt and 500 ml (17 fl oz/2 cups) water in a saucepan over medium heat until just about to boil. Stirring continuously with a wooden spoon, gradually sift in the buckwheat flour until thick and smooth. Continue to stir and cook until thickened and you have difficulty moving the spoon. Remove from the heat and transfer the mixture to the prepared tin, smoothing the surface evenly. Cover with a sheet of baking paper and refrigerate for 1–2 hours, until set.

Turn the slice out onto a clean work surface and cut into 3 cm (1¼ in) thick slices.

Heat the olive oil in a large frying pan over medium heat and, working in batches, fry the slices for 3 minutes each side, or until golden. Transfer to a plate and sprinkle both sides with the sugar. Serve immediately.

BRAÇ DE GITANO

GYPSY'S ARM

Known by many different names around the world, but commonly referred to as the Swiss roll, this cake is by no means indigenous to Catalunya, nor is it Swiss. The name 'gypsy's arm' may have come from a travelling monk who brought the cake back to Spain from Egypt, naming it the 'Egyptian's arm'. As the Spanish word for gypsy (gitano) is derived from 'egiptano' (Egyptian) it makes sense that the name changed over time to gypsy's arm. Another theory suggests that gypsies pedalling copper and metals through towns and villages were compensated for their work with this cake and would happily leave with their materials in one arm and the cake, comfortably resting along the elbow down to the wrist, in the other.

Whatever the origin, it still remains a huge Catalan favourite and this chocolate version can be found in pretty much every cake shop and bakery throughout the region.

Serves 10–12

butter, for greasing
200 g (7 oz) dark chocolate (70% cocoa solids)
80 ml (2½ fl oz/⅓ cup) espresso coffee
6 large eggs, separated
150 g (5½ oz) caster (superfine) sugar
2 tablespoons cacao powder
1 tablespoon pure icing (confectioners') sugar, plus extra for dusting
1 tablespoon Pedro Ximénez or sweet sherry
185 ml (6 fl oz/¾ cup) thickened (whipping) cream
1 teaspoon vanilla bean paste

Preheat the oven to 160°C (320°F) fan-forced. Line a 29 x 24 x 3 cm (11½ x 9½ x 1¼ in) Swiss roll (jelly roll) tin with greased baking paper.

Place the chocolate and espresso in a heatproof bowl over simmering water. Stir until melted and smooth, then remove from the heat and set aside to cool slightly.

Using a stand mixer with the whisk attachment or electric beaters, beat the egg yolks and sugar until fluffy and pale. Fold through the melted chocolate and coffee mixture until well combined.

In a separate bowl, beat the egg whites to soft peaks, then gently fold through the chocolate and egg mixture.

Pour onto the prepared tray and bake for 12–15 minutes, until cooked through. Turn the oven off, leave the tray inside and keep the oven door slightly ajar to let the moisture escape. Allow the cake to cool in the oven for 10–15 minutes.

Combine the cacao powder and icing sugar in a small bowl, then sprinkle onto a sheet of baking paper just larger than the cooked sponge. Turn the sponge out onto the prepared baking paper and peel off the top piece of paper. Allow to cool completely, then sprinkle over the alcohol.

Whip the cream and vanilla bean paste in a bowl until firm, then evenly spread it over the sponge. Roll up the sponge, using the edges of the baking paper as a guide. Wrap the gypsy's arm in plastic wrap and refrigerate for 1–2 hours before slicing and serving.

BUNYOLS DE QUARESMA

ANISEED LENT DOUGHNUTS

These doughnuts are also known as 'bunyols de vent' (wind doughnuts) for their light, airy centres. This recipe is the Empordà version, spiced with aniseed and coriander. The 'bunyols' are traditionally only eaten during Lent, but these days you'll see them sold all year round. You can't just stop at one!

Give me a 'bunyol' and a coffee over a 'churro' with chocolate any day!

Makes about 60

300 ml (10 fl oz) full-cream (whole) milk, warmed

10 g (⅓ oz) fresh yeast (or 2 teaspoons dried yeast granules)

100 g (3½ oz) caster (superfine) sugar

500 g (1 lb 2 oz) plain (all-purpose) flour, plus extra for dusting

1 apple, peeled and cored, finely grated

2 tablespoons aniseed

1 tablespoon coriander seeds, ground

¼ teaspoon fine salt

80 g (2¾ oz) butter, softened

3 whole eggs

peel of 1 lemon

1.5 litres (51 fl oz/6 cups) oil, for deep-frying

100 ml (3½ fl oz) anise liqueur, such as pernod, Anis del mono or ouzo

100 g (3½ fl oz) granulated sugar

Whisk the milk, yeast and a pinch of the caster sugar in a jug. Set aside for 10 minutes in a warm place.

Place the caster sugar, flour, apple, aniseed, ground coriander seeds, salt, butter, eggs and lemon peel in the bowl of a stand mixer fitted with the flat beater paddle attachment. With the motor running on medium speed, gradually pour the milk and yeast mixture into the bowl and mix for 2–4 minutes, until you have a smooth, elastic dough.

Tip the dough into a large bowl, cover with plastic wrap and leave in a warm place to prove for about 1½ hours, until doubled in size.

Heat the oil in a large heavy-based saucepan to 190°C (370°F). Drop a pinch of dough into the oil – if it sizzles straight away the oil is ready (be careful not to let the oil become too hot, otherwise a crust will form around the doughnuts too quickly, leaving the centres raw and cold).

Fill a piping bag or large zip lock bag with the dough, snip off a corner and use scissors to cut short lengths of dough straight into the oil.

Working in batches, fry the doughnuts for 2–3 minutes each side, until golden. Transfer to a tray lined with paper towel to absorb the excess oil, then sprinkle with splashes of the liqueur. Transfer the doughnuts to a large bowl and toss with the granulated sugar while still warm.

Serve immediately with some sweet sherry, coffee or warm milk.

PIJAMA

PYJAMA TIME!

This dessert aims to offer a little bit of everything on the plate and you will find it on most hospitality menus throughout Catalunya. It's said to have been created in the 1950s by one of the most prestigious and oldest restaurants in Barcelona – 7 Portes – for the American soldiers who came into port and often requested a peach melba dessert. For me, the most famous version can be found at Els Quatre Gats – Picasso's hangout and where many visitors heading to the Picasso museum drop in to indulge.

Like many restaurants do nowadays, you can also cheat and buy ready-made flans or crème caramels, use tinned peaches, glacé cherries, whipped cream out of a tin and 'nueles' – the traditional Catalan Christmas wafer cigars. The quality of the ingredients isn't as important as the theatre of the dish and the look on children's faces when it comes to the table!

Serves 6

200 ml (7 fl oz) thickened (whipping) cream
2 tablespoons pure icing (confectioners') sugar
½ teaspoon almond extract
3 peaches
½ pineapple, peeled, cored and cut into 6 long wedges
80 g (2¾ oz) maraschino cherries
6 chocolate wafer cigars

Flans

300 g (10½ oz) caster (superfine) sugar
1 teaspoon lemon juice
500 ml (17 fl oz/2 cups) full-cream (whole) milk
½ cinnamon stick
½ teaspoon vanilla bean paste
3 eggs
2 egg yolks
boiling water

Using electric beaters, whip the cream, icing sugar and almond extract in a bowl for 3 minutes, until soft peaks form. Cover and chill in the fridge.

Preheat the oven to 160°C (320°F) fan-forced. To make the flans, place six 60 ml (2 fl oz/¼ cup) dariole or flan moulds in a deep baking dish.

Heat 100 g (3½ oz) of the sugar, the lemon juice and 3 tablespoons water in a small heavy-based saucepan over medium–high heat. Allow the mixture to bubble for 8–10 minutes, until golden. Very carefully pour the caramel into the base of the moulds. Set aside.

Heat the milk, cinnamon stick and vanilla bean paste in a saucepan over medium–low heat. When steaming and just about to boil, remove from the heat and set aside to steep for 20 minutes.

Whisk the eggs, egg yolks and remaining sugar in a large bowl. Strain the milk through a fine sieve into the egg mixture and stir until well combined. Pour into the moulds, leaving a 3 mm (⅛ in) gap at the top of each mould.

Pour enough boiling water into the baking dish to come three-quarters of the way up the sides of the moulds. Carefully transfer to the oven and bake for 45 minutes. Place the moulds on a wire rack to cool slightly before refrigerating for 3–4 hours, until completely set.

Meanwhile, score each peach with a cross at its base. Bring a saucepan of water to the boil and blanch the peaches for 3–4 minutes, until the skins start to peel away. Drain and plunge the peaches into iced water to refresh. Peel the peaches, cut in half and discard the stones.

Place the chilled cream in a piping bag with a star nozzle.

Invert the flans onto serving plates and position just left of centre. Pipe cream to one side and add a peach half and pineapple wedge. Place the cherries on top of the cream and poke in a wafer cigar.

PA DE PESSIC AL MICR°ONES

MICROWAVE SPONGE CAKE

Another modernist technique to come out of Catalunya, this time by pastry chef Albert Adrià (brother of Ferran), is the microwave sponge cake. By transferring the batter to a siphon, the whipped egg whites produce a foam with large air pockets, resulting in a super-fluffy, moist, easy and speedy recipe that you can add any sweet or savoury flavour to. Restaurant El Bulli quickly spread this innovation around the world through its army of humble, loyal chefs with a black sesame and miso flavour combination. You can blend two tablespoons of any fruit pulp you like into the batter, such as raspberry, passionfruit, banana or cherry, but I've stuck to a classic vanilla and used a hand-held blender instead of a nitrous oxide-charged siphon with an adjusted egg-to-flour ratio for a perfect result.

Serves 6

80 g (2¾ oz) butter, softened
80 g (2¾ oz) caster (superfine) sugar
1 egg
2 egg whites
60 ml (2 fl oz/¼ cup) full-cream (whole) milk
½ teaspoon vanilla bean paste
80 g (2¾ oz) self-raising flour
small pinch of salt

Cream the butter and sugar in a medium bowl using a whisk. Whisk in the egg and egg whites, then add the milk and vanilla bean paste. Fold in the flour and salt using a wooden spoon until you have a smooth, loose batter. Blitz for 2–3 minutes with a hand-held blender until bubbling and aerated.

Transfer the batter to six 110 ml (4 fl oz) plastic dariole moulds, cover tightly with plastic wrap and pierce two small holes to allow the steam to escape. Place in the centre of a microwave oven and cook on high for 1½ minutes.

The sponge cakes make a great addition to the macerated strawberries on page 192 or roughly torn up into chunks and stirred through the Macedonian fruit salad on page 194.

TORTELL DE REIS

THREE KINGS' CAKE

In Catalunya, the story of the Three Wise Men's visit to the baby Jesus on the Twelfth Day of Christmas is almost celebrated more than Christmas itself, especially for children who also receive gifts on this day. This morning tea cake – decorated on top with candied fruit to mimic the kings' 'jewels' – is served on the twelfth day and always contains a hidden coin or trinket for the lucky recipient and a dried kidney bean for the person who must be in charge of making the cake the following year. It's also a big tradition in Mexico where they hide a baby Jesus figurine inside the cake instead, representing a safe place for the birth of Jesus.

Serves 12

250 ml (8½ fl oz/1 cup) full-cream (whole) milk

30 g (1 oz) fresh yeast or 2 x 7 g (¼ oz) sachets dried yeast granules

150 g (5½ oz) caster (superfine) sugar

600 g (1 lb 5 oz) baker's flour, plus extra for dusting

1 teaspoon salt

3 eggs

200 g (7 oz) butter, softened, plus extra for greasing

1½ tablespoons orange blossom water

zest of 1 lemon

zest of 1 orange

75 g (2½ oz/½ cup) blanched almonds, toasted and finely chopped, plus 15 whole blanched almonds

2 tablespoons raw (demerara) sugar

oil spray

100 g (3½ oz) pearl (nib) sugar

6–8 slices candied fruit, such as figs, cherries or cedro

whipped cream or custard, to serve

Warm the milk in a saucepan to 30–35°C (85–95°F) using a kitchen thermometer to assist you. Stir the yeast into the warm milk until completely dissolved, then add 1 teaspoon of the caster sugar.

Place the remaining caster sugar, flour and salt in the bowl of a stand mixer fitted with the dough hook attachment. Mix on medium–low speed until evenly combined. Add two of the eggs and mix until incorporated, then add 170 g (6 oz) of the butter and mix well before finally adding the warm milk mixture, orange blossom water and both zests. Keep mixing for 2–3 minutes, until you have a smooth dough. (Add another tablespoon of flour if you feel the dough needs a little more to help bring it away from the side of the bowl.)

Turn the dough out onto a clean, floured work surface. Flour your hands and knead the dough into a smooth ball. Add a little extra flour if the dough is too wet. Transfer the dough to a large greased bowl and flip to grease the entire ball. Cover with a clean damp tea towel and set aside for 1–1½ hours, until risen by one-third.

Transfer the dough back to a clean, lightly floured work surface and flatten out to a 80 cm x 15 cm (32 in x 6 in) rectangle. Spread with the remaining softened butter, then sprinkle over the finely chopped almonds and raw sugar. Hide a kidney bean and a heatproof figurine in the dough, if you like. Roll the dough into a long cylinder, then curve the two ends round to meet each other and seal by pinching the dough together. Place on a lined baking tray, seam side down.

Roll up a ball of aluminium foil and spray with oil. Place it in the centre of the ring to maintain the shape. Set aside to prove for a further 1 hour.

Preheat the oven to 180°C (350°F).

Lightly beat the remaining egg in a small bowl and brush all over the dough. Decorate the dough with the pearl sugar, whole almonds and candied fruit, then bake for 35 minutes, or until starting to colour.

Remove from the oven, discard the foil and leave to cool on a wire rack. Serve with whipped cream or custard.

COCA DE SANT JOAN I CABELL D'ÀNGEL

SAINT JOAN CAKE

This delicious cake is traditionally eaten during the Spanish midsummer celebration of 'La revetlla de Sant Joan' (Saint John's Eve). Here, I've included my favourite filling: a sweetened spaghetti squash jam that you often find over on the Balearic Islands and used to fill 'ensaïmada' – a local Mallorcan pastry.

Serves 10–12

Cabell d'angel
1 spaghetti squash, cut in half lengthways, seeds removed
350 g (12½ oz) caster (superfine) sugar
zest of ½ lemon
juice of 1 lemon

Coca
250 ml (8½ fl oz/1 cup) full-cream (whole) milk
30 g (1 oz) fresh yeast or 2 x 7 g (¼ oz) sachets dried yeast granules
220 g (8 oz) caster (superfine) sugar
600 g (1 lb 5 oz) baker's flour, plus extra for dusting
1 teaspoon salt
3 eggs
170 g (6 oz) butter, softened, plus extra for greasing
30 ml (1 fl oz) dark rum
zest of 1 lemon
80 g (2¾ oz/½ cup) pine nuts
4–6 candied orange slices

To make the cabell d'angel, preheat the oven to 200°C (400°F). Line a baking tray with baking paper. Place the squash, flesh side down, on the prepared baking tray and bake for 30 minutes, or until the skin starts to soften. Allow to cool slightly, then scoop the flesh into a saucepan. Add the sugar, lemon zest and juice and gently cook over medium–low heat, stirring regularly, for 20–25 minutes, until all the sugar has dissolved. Set aside in a bowl to cool.

To make the coca, warm the milk in a saucepan to 30–35°C (85–95°F) using a kitchen thermometer to assist you. Stir the yeast into the warm milk until completely dissolved, then add 1 teaspoon of the caster sugar.

Place 150 g (5½ oz) of the caster sugar, the flour and salt in the bowl of a stand mixer fitted with the dough hook attachment. Mix on medium–low speed until evenly combined. Add two of the eggs and mix well, then incorporate the butter followed by the warm milk mixture, rum and lemon zest. Keep mixing for 3–5 minutes, until you have a smooth dough. (Add another tablespoon of flour if you feel the dough needs a little more to help bring it away from the side of the bowl.)

Turn the dough out onto a clean, floured work surface and knead into a smooth ball. Add a little extra flour if the dough is too wet and not elastic enough. Transfer the dough to a large greased bowl and flip to grease the entire ball. Cover with a clean damp tea towel and set aside for 1–1½ hours, until it has risen by one-third of its size.

Transfer the dough back to a lightly floured work surface and divide into two even-sized balls. Line two baking trays with baking paper and flatten the dough into two 30 cm x 20 cm (12 in x 8 in) rectangles on the trays. Spread the cooled squash jam over one of the dough rectangles, leaving a 2 cm (¾ in) border around the edge. Place the other rectangle over the jam and press the edges to seal. Set aside to prove for a further 30 minutes in a warm draught-free place.

Preheat the oven to 180°C (350°F).

Whisk the remaining egg and brush all over the dough. Combine the remaining sugar with 1 teaspoon water to make a rough paste. Decorate the dough with the pine nuts and candied orange slices, then dot the sugar over the cake.

Bake for 35 minutes, then remove from the oven and leave to cool on a wire rack before tucking in.

CODONYAT I FORMATGE

QUINCE PASTE & MANCHEGO

This is surely one of the greatest combinations – home-made quince paste and semi-firm manchego. Eat it as a snack or even for breakfast to get you going. You can use quince paste as a jam to fill pastries and cakes, loosen it down with boiling water to make a sauce or spread it on toast with melted cheese on top, to get you through the winter months. It also goes without saying that quince paste is the perfect addition to any cheese board, plus it keeps for months.

Makes about 1 kg (2 lb 3 oz)

2 kg (4 lb 6 oz) quince, washed, peeled, cored and cut into wedges (reserve the peel from 2 quinces)
2 large strips of lemon peel
½ teaspoon vanilla bean paste
1 kg (2 lb 3 oz) caster (superfine) sugar
3 tablespoons fresh lemon juice
oil spray
manchego or your favourite cheese, to serve

Place the quince in a large heavy-based saucepan and add enough cold water to cover the fruit by 2 cm (¾ in). Tie the quince peel in a square of muslin (cheesecloth) – this gives a richer colour and maximises the pectin – and add to the pan, along with the lemon peel and vanilla. Bring to the boil over medium–high heat, then reduce to a simmer, cover and cook for 30–40 minutes, until the fruit is tender.

Strain the quince and discard the quince peel, then transfer to a blender and blitz the fruit and the lemon peel to a smooth purée.

Return the purée to a clean non-stick saucepan and heat over medium–low heat. Add the sugar and stir through until dissolved, then add the lemon juice. Reduce the heat to as low as it can go and cook, stirring regularly, for 1½–2 hours, until thickened and starting to turn a rich burnt-orange, maroon colour.

Lightly spray a 23 cm (9 in) square tin with oil and line with baking paper or plastic wrap. Spoon the quince paste into the tin and smooth the surface using a rubber spatula.

Refrigerate for a minimum of 4 hours until set, before cutting into thick slices or triangles to serve with your favourite cheese.

Wrap the left-over quince paste in baking paper and plastic wrap and keep in the fridge for up to 2 months.

PERES AMB VI DE PRIORAT I GELAT DE SAFRÀ

RED WINE-POACHED PEARS & SAFFRON ICE CREAM

Most of Spain's pears are grown in the Ebro Valley. South of the valley is the protected Priorat wine region, which produces excellent dry, minerally, earthy grapes used to make red varieties of Garnacha and Carignan, which match perfectly with the pears.

This saffron ice cream takes me straight back to Catalunya where saffron has been widely exported since the 15th century. Its earthy, floral, musky taste paired with the richness of the anglaise ice cream and sharpness of the wine, make this dessert absolute bliss.

Serves 4

4 corella or williams pears
peel and juice of 1 lemon
1 litre (34 fl oz/4 cups) dry red wine
1 cinnamon stick
1 vanilla bean, split in half lengthways
150 g (5½ oz) caster (superfine) sugar
1 fresh bay leaf

Saffron ice cream
500 ml (17 fl oz/2 cups) full-cream (whole) milk
2 pinches of saffron
2 tablespoons floral honey
5 egg yolks
80 g (2¾ oz) caster (superfine) sugar
1 teaspoon cornflour (cornstarch)
½ teaspoon vanilla bean paste
200 g (7 oz) crème fraîche

To make the ice cream, heat the milk and saffron in a saucepan over medium–high heat until just about to simmer. Stir through the honey and set aside.

Whisk the egg yolks in a heatproof bowl, then whisk through the sugar, cornflour and vanilla bean paste until thick and pale. Gradually whisk the warm milk into the egg mixture, then place over a saucepan of simmering water. Cook, stirring, for about 12 minutes, until the mixture thickens and coats the back of a wooden spoon, then strain through a fine sieve while still hot.

Allow to cool completely, then whisk through the crème fraîche. Set aside in the fridge for 4 hours or preferably overnight.

Line a 21 cm x 11 cm (8¼ in x 4¼ in) loaf (bar) tin with baking paper and place in the freezer to chill.

Churn the custard in an ice cream machine according to the manufacturer's instructions until thick and smooth. Scrape into the chilled loaf tin and freeze for 2 hours.

Peel the pears from the stalk down to the base, leaving the stalk intact. Place in a bowl and cover with cold water. Add the lemon juice.

Place the lemon peel, wine, cinnamon stick, vanilla, sugar and bay leaf in a medium saucepan over medium–high heat and stir to dissolve the sugar. Bring to the boil, then reduce the heat to a gentle simmer. Strain the pears and lower into the simmering wine mixture.

Cut a circle of baking paper the same diameter as the pan and place it over the pears. If the pears continue to float, weigh them down with a small plate or bowl to completely submerge them under the liquid. Cook for 12–15 minutes, until softened.

Serve the pears with a little of their poaching liquid and two scoops of the saffron ice cream.

SALSES I BROUS

SAUCES
& BROTHS

Sauces and stocks are an integral part of the Catalan kitchen. Other Spanish cuisines might not require a standalone chapter for recipes that are simply incorporated into other dishes, but these guys deserve their own space as they are the very foundation of Catalunya's gastronomy.

The main base sauces are the 'picada' and 'sofregit', and they provide structure, flavour, stability, texture and consistency to any number of dishes. 'Sofregit' is added at the start of cooking, slowly caramelising ingredients together to make a rich, jam-like base for many rice, meat, vegetable and seafood recipes. 'Picada', on the other hand, is used at the end of cooking as a seasoning to give body, depth and thickness to a dish.

The stocks and broths that hail out of Catalunya vary from cook to cook, but tend to be quite distinct from that of their more strict culinary cousins in France. Both chicken and fish stocks are also used as broths, light bases for soups themselves with the inclusion of rice, pasta, legumes, additional proteins and vegetables.

'Fumet de peix' or simply 'fumet' is an opaque, colourless fish-stock base with a clean and delicate taste of the sea. It's used as a flavoursome hydrator in many regional seafood dishes, such as Suquet de peix (page 102), Arròs negre (page 107) and Rossejat (page 112). Similarly, the famous Catalan 'mar i muntanya' chicken and scampi recipe (page 151) would not be the same without its 'brou' (broth). Beef stock, however, is used simply as a base for other sauces, such as the Salsa española (page 249) or in stews and braises, such as the umami delight of Fricandò (page 134) or the Caldareta (page 146).

Finally, this chapter also features condiments, such as 'allioli' and 'maionesa', and the salsas 'julivert', 'almadroc', romesco and 'salvitxada', integral sauces that emphasise and delicately harmonise with their accompanying dish.

ALBERGÍNIA
I NºUS

EGGPLANT & WALNUT SAUCE

When they're in peak season from midsummer to autumn, eggplants (aubergines) have a firm glossy skin and creamy flesh. They're like sponges, which is fantastic for absorbing flavour, but less so for absorbing oil, so I like to salt them first before cooking.

This rich, versatile relish-cum-sauce-cum-stuffing-cum-condiment or dip can be served at breakfast, lunch or dinner and is great to have hanging around your fridge when you need something to complement a summer meal or a snack solution to take down to the beach. It can also be used as a vegan bolognese or thick stuffing for cannelloni or capsicums (bell peppers). Alternatively, serve with a fried egg on toast or alongside your favourite pan-fried protein for dinner.

Cooking in clay or terracotta is quite traditional in Catalunya and this is the perfect dish to use this method, as all the cooking is done over an even medium heat.

Makes about 550 g (1 lb 3 oz)

400 g (14 oz) tomatoes
2 large eggplants (aubergines),
    sliced into 1 cm (½ in) thick
    rounds
2 tablespoons sea salt
125 ml (4 fl oz/½ cup) olive oil
1 medium onion, finely grated
2 garlic cloves, finely grated
35 g (1¼ oz/⅓ cup) walnuts
250 ml (8½ fl oz/1 cup) vegetable
    stock
salt flakes and freshly cracked
    black pepper
1½ tablespoons chopped parsley

Score a small cross in the base of each tomato. Bring a medium saucepan of water to the boil, lower in the tomatoes and boil for 3–4 minutes, until the skins start to peel away. Drain and plunge the tomatoes into iced water to stop the cooking process. Once cool, peel away the skins and discard. Roughly chop the tomatoes and set aside in a bowl.

Place the eggplant in a colander with a bowl underneath and toss with the sea salt. Stand for 10 minutes, then rinse under cold water and pat dry with paper towel.

Heat half the olive oil in a frying pan over medium–high heat. Working in batches, fry the eggplant for 4 minutes on each side, or until golden. Remove from the heat and set aside. Heat the remaining oil in an earthenware pot or frying pan over medium heat. Add the onion and garlic, along with a pinch of salt and fry for 15 minutes, or until the onion is soft and caramelised. Add the tomato and simmer for 10 minutes, or until the liquid has slightly reduced, then add the eggplant. Continue to cook, stirring occasionally, for 20–30 minutes, until the eggplant slices start to fall apart in the sauce.

Coarsely blitz the walnuts in the small bowl of a food processor, then add to the pot along with the vegetable stock. Season to taste, then reduce the heat to low and cook until the sauce is reduced and thick. Stir through the parsley.

Serve the sauce in its earthenware pot or transfer to a serving bowl. The sauce will keep in an airtight container in the fridge for up to 10 days.

SALSA ALMADROC

MEDIEVAL CHEESE DIP

This medieval cheese and garlic sauce emulsified with egg is making a bit of a comeback. It can be served hot or cold and, depending on its consistency, it can be used to fill ravioli, stuff calamari, drizzled over a bowl of pasta or loosened down further and used as a dressing.

For this version, I wanted to create a more traditional sauce with a condiment texture to serve with meat and fish, but I soon discovered it's just as good on toast or served as a dip with crudités. I've used two types of cheese here – the goat's curd gives acidity and a creamy texture, while the aged sheep's cheese provides a salty, mineral-rich flavour.

Serves 4

2 hardboiled eggs
150 g (5½ oz) goat's curd or chèvre, roughly chopped
150 g (5½ oz) aged manchego or pecorino, roughly chopped
1 garlic clove, minced
pinch of salt flakes
60 ml (2 fl oz/¼ cup) extra virgin olive oil
2 tablespoons sparkling mineral water

Separate the egg whites and yolks and set the yolks aside. Place the egg whites and remaining ingredients in a food processor and blitz until smooth.

Transfer to a serving bowl and finely grate the egg yolk over the top.

SALSA SALVITXADA I SALSA ROMESCO

RED PEPPER SAUCE

Some people claim that romesco and salvitxada are the same sauce, just identified differently depending on what they are accompanied with: salvitxada is only ever served with Calçots (see page 58), while romesco is an integral part of the coastal winter salad Xató (see page 33). Others argue that salvitxada does not contain bread and that this is the difference. I've included two recipes here for argument's sake, but every village and household has their way – some like it with a lot of vinegar while others like it strong in garlic. The variations are endless, so mix and match to suit your own taste.

Each sauce makes 750 ml (25½ fl oz/3 cups)

Salsa salvitxada
4 ripe medium tomatoes
100 g (3½ oz) blanched almonds, toasted
50 g (1¾ oz) roasted hazelnuts
1 garlic clove, peeled
1 tablespoon sherry vinegar
2–3 dried ñora peppers, rehydrated in hot water, seeds removed and flesh scraped from skins (see note)
1 teaspoon sea salt
½ teaspoon freshly cracked black pepper
100 ml (3½ fl oz) extra virgin olive oil

Salsa romesco
1 garlic bulb, cut in half crossways, plus 1 garlic clove, peeled
sea salt
2 medium tomatoes
1 red capsicum (bell pepper)
½ white onion, unpeeled
1 piece thickly sliced bread
2 tablespoons sherry vinegar
40 g (1½ oz/¼ cup) blanched almonds, toasted
35 g (1¼ oz) roasted hazelnuts
2 teaspoons sweet pimentón
80 ml (2½ fl oz/⅓ cup) extra virgin olive oil
freshly cracked black pepper

To make the salsa salvitxada, heat a barbecue grill plate to high. Blister the tomatoes until the skins peel away. Peel and discard the skins.

Blitz the nuts in a food processor, then add the garlic, vinegar, pepper flesh, salt, pepper and peeled tomatoes. Blitz again then, with the motor running, slowly add the oil until well combined. Incorporate a little water if you prefer a thinner consistency. The sauce will keep in an airtight container in the fridge for 4–5 days.

To make the salsa romesco, preheat the oven to 200°C (400°F) fan-forced.

Place the garlic on a sheet of foil and sprinkle with salt. Wrap the garlic in the foil and bake for 30–40 minutes, until caramelised and the cloves are popping up out of their skins. Set aside to cool, then squeeze the roasted garlic flesh into a bowl.

Heat a barbecue grill plate to high and char the tomato, capsicum and onion until the skins start to burn slightly and moisture begins to seep out. Remove from the heat, place the capsicum in a small bowl and cover with plastic wrap. Peel the tomato and onion.

Toast the bread in a frying pan or on the grill plate, then rub the remaining garlic clove over the toast – the coarseness of the bread will grate the garlic along its surface. Transfer to a shallow bowl and soak the bread in the sherry vinegar and 1 tablespoon water.

Peel and deseed the capsicum, then place it in a blender with the tomato, onion, soaked toast, roasted garlic, nuts, pimentón and 1 teaspoon salt. Blitz until well combined then, with the motor running, slowly pour in the oil. Incorporate a little water if you would like a thinner consistency and season to taste with black pepper. The sauce will keep in an airtight container in the fridge for 4–5 days.

Note: The earthy, bittersweet flavour of salvitxada comes from the dried ñora pepper. As they're not readily available or easy to source outside of Catalunya, you can substitute dried Mexican peppers, such as ancho, mulato or pasilla. Failing that, add 1 teaspoon of good-quality sweet pimentón.

PICADA

CATALAN-STYLE PESTO

Picada is essentially a fresh paste used at the end of the cooking process to add texture, depth of flavour and an extra dimension to otherwise simple peasant dishes.

There are a few picadas in the Catalan repertoire and many, such as this one, can be adapted to match what you're serving it with. Toasted saffron threads can be added to accompany fish dishes, chocolate to deepen meat braises, while the nut combinations can be changed for pine nuts, pistachio nuts or even toasted pepitas (pumpkin seeds) for a more modern twist, along with different types of herbs and spices.

This recipe is my standard go-to, which I play around with from time to time, depending on the ultimate result I'm looking for.

Makes 250 ml (8½ fl oz/1 cup)

2 tablespoons extra virgin olive oil, plus extra for drizzling

3 garlic cloves, finely chopped

2 thin slices white bread or baguette, cut into small cubes

40 g (1½ oz/¼ cup) blanched almonds, toasted

35 g (1¼ oz/¼ cup) hazelnuts, roasted, skins rubbed off

½ teaspoon mild chilli powder (optional)

Heat the olive oil in a frying pan over medium heat and sauté the garlic and bread for 6–8 minutes, until golden.

Place the nuts, chilli powder, if using, garlic and bread in a food processor. With the motor running, drizzle in a little olive oil and blend until you have a thick, sticky paste.

Stir the picada through any number of the dishes in this book, or use it to thicken your favourite winter stew.

The picada will keep in an airtight container in the fridge for up to 10 days.

Albergínia i nous

Salsa de julivert

Salsa romesco

Picada

Salsa almadroc

SALSA DE JULIVERT

SALSA VERDE

Julivert is the Catalan word for parsley and this quick little dressing that's been around since medieval times can be put on top of almost anything, from pan-fried fish and large cuts of roasted meats to grilled vegetables, or even used as a base for vinaigrettes.

For me, curly-leaf parsley works better here as it has a much earthier flavour and less moisture than its flat-leaf cousin. You can use any other herbs you like with the parsley – chervil is fantastic if you can get it.

Some recipes include bread and almonds as well, but I like to leave them out to keep the salsa lighter and more versatile as an accompaniment. My mother-in-law used to keep a bottle of left-over Cava in the fridge door and add any unfinished last drops of a variety of white wines to use in this salsa. She'd add to it, use it, add to it, use it – the same bottle for years! It was the best version I've ever had.

Makes 375 ml (12½ fl oz/1½ cups)

3 small garlic cloves
pinch of sea salt
1 bunch curly-leaf parsley,
   leaves chopped
2 sprigs chervil, marjoram or
   oregano, leaves chopped
3–4 mint leaves, finely chopped
2 teaspoons dry white wine (or
   1 teaspoon white wine vinegar)
80 ml (2½ fl oz/⅓ cup) light-tasting
   extra virgin olive oil
60 ml (2 fl oz/¼ cup) grapeseed
   or sunflower oil
salt flakes and freshly cracked
   black pepper

Using a mortar and pestle, pound the garlic with the salt to a paste. Add the herbs, one by one, and lightly bruise them into the garlic between each addition. Pour in the wine or vinegar and gently pound into the herbs, then gradually add the oils, stirring around the mortar to incorporate. Season to taste and serve straight away, or even better let it sit for a few hours before using.

You can also make this salsa in a food processor on pulse, but you don't want it to be a homogenised pesto-looking sauce. It's nice when the herbs pool in the liquid a little when you drizzle it over your favourite dish.

Salsa julivert will keep in the fridge for 1–2 days.

SºFREGIT

SOFRITO

This sauce is the base, the backbone, the primrose path to braises, sautés and various paellas. Make a large batch, portion it up and keep it on hand in the freezer to add depth of flavour to your favourite dishes.

Figueres onions (or pink onions) are a favourite to use for 'sofregit', but in lieu of these not being readily available outside of Catalunya, you can use white or brown onions or a mixture of white, brown and red. The finer the cut the better – you can even coarsely grate them or pulse them in a food processor if you are making a big batch, just be careful you don't end up with onion soup.

Roma (plum) tomatoes are the first choice here, which are fleshy and juicy. Any ripe, mature red tomato will do, though. These are also best grated, but if you're pressed for time or want to make this in the middle of winter and can't access ripe tomatoes, then you can use the same weight in tinned chopped or diced tomatoes.

Makes about 850 g (1 lb 14 oz)

300 ml (10 fl oz) extra virgin olive oil
4 medium onions, peeled and finely diced
1½ teaspoons salt
6 garlic cloves, finely grated
800 g (1 lb 12 oz) roma (plum) tomatoes, coarsely grated, skins discarded
250 ml (8½ fl oz/1 cup) dry sherry

Heat the oil in a large heavy-based saucepan or paella pan over medium heat. Add the onion and stir through the oil. Allow to simmer, then reduce the heat to medium–low and cook, stirring often, for about 10 minutes, until the onion is translucent. Add the salt and continue to gently cook the onion, stirring, for a further 15 minutes, until golden. Add the garlic and cook for another 15 minutes, until all the moisture has evaporated and only the caramelised onion, garlic and oil are left in the pan.

Add the grated tomato and increase the heat to medium until the mixture starts to simmer. Continue to cook for 30 minutes, stirring the sofregit, as it reduces and the liquid evaporates. Reduce the heat to low and cover, stirring occasionally, for 20–30 minutes, until the sauce starts to turn a dark golden, chocolatey colour. Remove the lid, add the sherry and increase the heat to medium–high for the last 5 minutes of cooking, until all the alcohol has been absorbed.

Set aside to cool completely. Store in an airtight container in the fridge for up to 2 weeks or divide into portions and store in the freezer for up to 2 months.

ALLIOLI

AÏOLI

The Catalans love this sauce as much as the Americans love their ketchup and the French their mustard. It is an essential at the table no matter what's on offer: seafood stews, grilled prawns (shrimp), squid-ink dishes, dry-roasted meats, the list goes on.

Here, I've included three versions of this famous condiment, so experiment and see which one you like best. The traditional method requires no egg and is simply an emulsification of garlic (all) and (i) oil (oli), but it demands patience and will-power; the suave uses cooked garlic making it a little easier to digest, while the moderna is perfect for those who are simply short on time and equipment.

Each recipe makes 125 g (4½ oz/½ cup)

Traditional
5 garlic cloves, peeled, germ removed, thinly sliced
½ teaspoon sea salt
½ teaspoon lemon juice
60 ml (2 fl oz/¼ cup) light-tasting olive oil

Suave
1 garlic bulb
pinch of sea salt
1 egg yolk, at room temperature
125 ml (4 fl oz/½ cup) extra virgin olive oil
½ teaspoon lemon juice

Moderna
125 g (4½ oz/½ cup) whole egg mayonnaise
3 garlic cloves, minced or finely grated
⅓ teaspoon salt
½ teaspoon sherry vinegar

To make the traditional, pound the garlic and salt using a mortar and pestle to a fine, wet paste. Squeeze in the lemon juice and mix to combine. Gradually add the oil, ½ teaspoon at a time, mixing and pulverising vigorously until completely combined. Add a splash of water at the end if you would like it a little runnier.

To make the suave, preheat the oven to 190°C (375°F) fan-forced.

Cut the top 5 mm (¼ in) off the garlic head, to expose the cloves. Sprinkle with salt and wrap tightly in foil. Bake for 25–30 minutes, until the garlic is caramelised and the cloves are popping up out of their skins. Allow to cool, then turn upside down and squeeze the flesh into a mortar and pestle or small bowl. Mix through the salt, then add the egg and mix through to combine. Gradually whisk in the oil, 1 teaspoon at a time, until you have a smooth paste. Season with the lemon juice.

To make the moderna, place all the ingredients in a bowl and mix until thoroughly combined.

Keep the allioli in an airtight container in the fridge for 3–4 days.

MAI♀NESA

MAYONNAISE

Around the time of the 1992 Olympics the use of raw egg yolk was banned in hospitality outlets. Instead of teaching people how to properly handle and store fresh mayonnaise, pasteurised, liquidised egg yolks were invented and sold in tetra brik cartons, which are still used today. Part of the pay off, I guess, is that Catalans have other more relaxed regulations, such as those that allow you to visit a bar filled with plates of beautifully displayed pintxos for your temptation, uncovered for you to help yourself.

Although not allowed in the hospitality world, you can still find some old-school restaurants and new-school modern chefs serving up mayo' the old way.

Makes 185 g (6½ oz/¾ cup)

1 egg yolk
1 whole egg
1 tablespoon sherry vinegar
pinch of salt
80 ml (2½ fl oz/⅓ cup)
　grapeseed oil
60 ml (2 fl oz/¼ cup) extra virgin
　olive oil

In a large bowl, whisk the egg yolk and egg, then incorporate the sherry vinegar and salt. Whisking continuously, gradually pour in the oils in a thin steady stream, until you have a thick mayonnaise. Alternatively, you can make the mayonnaise in the small bowl of a food processor or with a hand-held blender.

Keep the maionesa in an airtight container in the fridge for 3–4 days.

FUMET DE PEIX

FISH STOCK

It's typical to see 'peix de roca' (small rock fish) varieties piled up in huge mounds at the market for making 'fumet' (stock). This combination of whole non-oily, small-boned fish, with internals that haven't quite developed yet, make for a clean, sweet result.

The heads and bones of larger white-fleshed non-oily fish, such as monkfish, cod or red mullet and snapper are then mixed into the pot with the baby fish to add a saltier, fishier depth of flavour.

It's important not to overcook your fish stock. You want to extract the gelatine and flavour without leaching too much from the actual bones, which are more delicate than animal bones and can transfer a bitter taste to your stock when cooked for a long time. It's, therefore, important to cut your vegetables into smaller pieces to allow for the shorter cooking time.

You can also add carrot, tomato and prawn (shrimp) or shellfish heads and shells to your stock for a sweeter flavour and deeper colour, especially if cooking paella. Alternatively, add them when reheating your stock to cook with, which is what I usually do.

Use this stock as a poaching liquid for delicate fish or for making quick broths and soups with the addition of some white-fleshed fish, chopped carrot, garlic and parsley – the Catalan Penicillin!!

Makes 4–5 litres (4¼–5¼ qts)

2 kg (4 lb 6 oz) large fish heads, bones, fins and tails (monkfish, cod, red mullet or snapper)
500 g (1 lb 2 oz) medium whole whitebait
2 tablespoons fine sea salt
1 leek, white part only, split in half lengthways, rinsed and sliced
2 brown onions, each chopped into 8 chunks
2 celery stalks, chopped into 3 cm (1¼ in) chunks
1 fresh bay leaf
8 white peppercorns
60 ml (2 fl oz/¼ cup) dry white wine
3 parsley sprigs

Soak the fish heads, bones, fins, tails and whitebait with the salt in a large bowl of cold water for 30 minutes. Drain and rinse well under cold running water, making sure you remove any blood from the larger spinal bones.

Transfer the fish to a large saucepan or stockpot with the remaining ingredients except the parsley and cover with 6 litres (6½ qts) cold water. Bring to a simmer and skim off any impurities that rise to the surface. Simmer for 20 minutes, then remove from the heat, add the parsley and allow to steep for 15 minutes.

Strain through a fine-mesh sieve and allow to cool completely.

Store in the fridge for 3–4 days or in the freezer in batches for up to 3 months.

BR°U DE POLLASTRE

CHICKEN BROTH

Drink this broth solo, or boil it up with some rice and extra garlic at the beginning of winter and you won't get sick all season, so says the old wives' tale.

Used as a stock, this broth can form the base of any dish requiring a liquid reduction. You can also turn it into a double chicken stock (roasted chicken bones added to the broth and reduced) for a richer, browner result or add jamón bones and off-cuts to make a super-tasty ham stock to cook your beans and pulses in.

Makes 3–4 litres (3–4¼ qts)

4 chicken frames, chopped in half

500 g (1 lb 2 oz) chicken wings or necks (or a mixture)

2 tablespoons fine sea salt

1 leek, white part only, split in half lengthways, rinsed and sliced

2 brown onions, quartered

2 celery stalks, chopped into 6 cm (2½ in) chunks

1 fresh bay leaf

2 sprigs thyme

8 white peppercorns

60 ml (2 fl oz/¼ cup) dry white wine

½ bunch parsley stalks

Soak the chicken frames, wings and/or necks with the salt in a large bowl of cold water for 30 minutes. Drain and rinse well under cold running water, removing any visible fat.

Place the chicken in a large saucepan or stockpot and cover with 6 litres (6½ qts) cold water. Bring to a simmer over medium heat and skim off any impurities that rise to the surface. Add the remaining ingredients, then reduce the heat to low and gently simmer for 2 hours, skimming the fat off regularly, then remove from the heat and allow to steep for a further 1 hour.

Strain through a fine-mesh sieve and allow to cool completely.

Store in the fridge for 3–4 days or in the freezer in batches for up to 3 months.

FONS FOSC DE CARN

BROWN STOCK

This stock owes its name to its dark colour, which is achieved by roasting bones and vegetables to caramelise the proteins and extract a richer, deeper flavour. It is an essential ingredient in Salsa Española (see opposite) and as a vegetable-thickened 'demi-glace' or mother sauce that's used throughout the culinary world in traditional French-schooled kitchens. It's also perfect for stews, casseroles and meat-based rice dishes.

The smaller the pieces of bone, the faster you'll extract the flavour and gelatine.

Makes 4 litres (4¼ qts)

4 kg (8 lb 13 oz) veal or lamb bones (or a mixture), sawn into 5 cm (2 in) pieces (ask your butcher to do this for you)
2 garlic bulbs, cut in half crossways
2 brown onions, halved
3 celery stalks, halved
2 carrots, quartered
2 tablespoons tomato paste (concentrated purée)
4 dried porcini mushrooms
2 fresh bay leaves
3 sprigs thyme
1 tablespoon black peppercorns
½ bunch parsley stalks
250 ml (8½ fl oz/1 cup) dry white wine

Thoroughly rinse the bones under cold running water. Set aside to air-dry on a clean tea towel.

Preheat the oven to 200°C (400°F) fan-forced.

Transfer the bones to a large roasting tin and roast for 30 minutes. Rotate the tin, then chuck in the garlic and give the bones a stir so they brown evenly. Cook for a further 30 minutes, or until the bones start to crisp and turn a dark golden colour. Add the vegetables and tomato paste, give everything another stir and roast for a further 40 minutes.

Transfer the roasted bones, garlic and vegetables to a large stockpot and cover with 8 litres (8½ qts) water. (Alternatively use half chicken stock and half water for a more decadent, richer result.) Add the dried porcini mushrooms, bay leaves, thyme, peppercorns and parsley stalks.

Place the roasting tin on the stovetop over medium–high heat and deglaze the tin with the white wine and 250 ml (8½ fl oz/1 cup) water, scraping up all the caramelised residual crispy bits from the bottom of the tin. Pour this mixture into the stockpot and slowly bring to a gentle boil, then reduce the heat to low and simmer for 4–6 hours, regularly skimming off any impurities that rise to the surface.

Remove from the heat and allow to steep for 1 hour before straining through a fine-mesh sieve. Allow to completely cool, then store in the fridge for 3–4 days or in the freezer in batches for up to 3 months.

Note: For an even richer stock to use for sauces, gravys or glazes, reduce the stock by another half over a very low simmer.

SALSA
ESPAÑOLA

SPANISH
SAUCE

A classic Spanish 'brown sauce' that's essentially used as a gravy or jus. It's fundamental in Spanish kitchens and is often served with beef fillet, steaks and roasts.

**Makes 750 ml (25½ fl oz/
3 cups)**

1½ tablespoons olive oil
1 brown onion, roughly chopped
1 carrot, roughly chopped
5 garlic cloves, smashed
2 tablespoons plain (all-purpose)
   flour
750 ml (25½ fl oz/3 cups) dry
   red wine
2 fresh bay leaves
4 sprigs thyme
6 sprigs parsley
4 dried morel mushrooms
1 field mushroom, roughly
   chopped
2 whole cloves
5 black peppercorns
1 litre (34 fl oz/4 cups) Fons fosc
   de carn (see opposite)
1 tablespoon sea salt
50 g (1¾ oz) butter

Heat a large heavy-based saucepan over medium–high heat. Add the olive oil, onion, carrot and garlic and cook, stirring occasionally, until the vegetables start to brown, then add the flour and cook out for 2–3 minutes, until well incorporated. Add the red wine and bring to a simmer. Reduce the heat to medium–low and cook until the wine has reduced by half. Stir through the herbs, mushrooms, cloves and peppercorns, then add the stock. Simmer gently for 40 minutes.

Using a fine-mesh sieve, strain the sauce into another large saucepan, pushing as much of the cooked vegetable pulp through the strainer as possible. Return the stock to a simmer and cook over low heat for about 30 minutes, until reduced by one-third and slightly thickened. Season with the salt and whisk through the butter just before serving.

Pour into a gravy jug and serve at the table with your favourite roast.

The sauce will keep in the fridge for 1–2 weeks or in the freezer in batches for up to 3 months.

GRÀCIES

It takes a village to raise a child and this book has a lot of very talented and special people to thank for its birth. First, thanks to the publishing family at Smith Street Books who are such a young, loving and adoptive tribe.

Paul McNally, founder of Smith Street Books – your vision, experience, respect, passion and trust for what we all do makes the creative process collaborative and easy; Lucy Heaver, publisher, editor, sister – this book wouldn't exist without your bright idea. I've broken new firsts with you there to hold my hand in this world and encouraging my voice; I can think of no one I'd rather help make this book; Daniel New, designer – thanks for really listening and achieving such an inspiring visual and original result that takes the reader right there to the fields, coastlines and streets of Catalunya; Heather Menzies, typesetter – super grateful to have had your expert eyes putting everything into place; Helena Holmgren, indexer – seriously, thank you – such an underestimated, skilled job, I really appreciate it; Rochelle Eagle, photographer – your gifted eyes see more than most and bring everything that's in front of you, including the not-so obvious, together in one piece. It's a real talent that you combine with patience, humour and hard work. Thank you for giving so much; Lee Blaylock, stylist – thanks for wanting to be a part of this and bringing all your heart and soul to everything you do. Your generosity and friendship to me over the years has always been abundant and real; Rachael Lane – I always learn so much from you. The precision, consistency and cohesion you bring on a daily basis really is integral to everything we do; Gabrielle Evans – guapa! Thanks so much for jumping into and onto everything you come across with skill and curiosity. It truly was so great working with you and having you on board the book train!!! Jason Rodwell – Chefffff!!! You're always there. Reliable, responsible, fun and inventive. Thanks for being there for the big stuff. You're the greatest mate any chef could wish for; and merci beaucoup to Josephine, too, for all your support.

Suppliers – thank you for giving me guidance and always having time for me in our busy worlds. Gary and Ash McBean, The Narduzzo family at Pino's, Anna Samiotis from Prahan Seafoods, Stella from D&J Chickens and to all their families and staff who are all so passionate and generous.

Personally – to my mum and dad and dear, dear friends Samantha Lane and Emma Bulpit. I couldn't have done these last 18 months without you to lean on, let alone write this book. Also thanks to Thomas Ryan, Anna Hancock, Eleanor Henderson and Martina Tuohey.

To my friend, chef, mentor and biggest supporter Karen Martini, thanks for everything you've shared with me; I wouldn't know a lot about how to make books and finding my own voice without being by your side for the last five years. Philippa Sibley, Karina Duncan, Armelle Habib, Peta Gray, Julia Busuttil Nishimura, Marnie Rowe, Judy Webb, Mary Small, Julie Rani Vecera – women of this industry, thank you for continuously inspiring, encouraging, believing and backing me. Also thanks to Matt Preston for really appreciating every aspect of what we all do and celebrating and promoting the culinary arts.

My Catalan families – thanks to Georgina Konstandakopoulos, The Triado sisters and all the Kasparo crew, Carlos Gil, My Mallorcan family and to The Rodriguez-Ponce family for having me in your lives for such a special and important time and always having me in your hearts.

To Morgan – thank you for your constant help and support through this whole process, for sharing our space to get the job done and always being there in the background, lending a helping hand. For letting me be me, for loving me and Doni doodles and for our new baby bundle. Moltes mercès a tots!

ABOUT THE AUTHOR

Emma Warren studied horticultural science before transferring her love of the veggie patch to the kitchen. She moved to Spain in 2001 and immersed herself in the world of Catalan cuisine. Splitting her time between Mallorca and Barcelona, she learned her first chef's skills at the popular café 'Kasparo', which focused on market-driven, seasonal local produce. Emma soon became head chef and ran the café for three years before returning home to Melbourne, Australia, to set up the kitchen 'Hogar Español' at the iconic Spanish Club on Johnston street in Fitzroy – a cult institution and live-music venue, where Spanish expats and local community came together.

Emma soon returned to Barcelona, where she ended up at Hotel Rey Don Jaime in the coastal town of Castelldefels, which became a major training ground for learning traditional Catalan cooking, culture and language. Back in Melbourne, Emma began working for some of Australia's most-respected chefs and helped Philipa Sibley set up the Albert Street Food and Wine Store. Today, she works closely with Karen Martini and Matt Preston at photoshoots, food festivals and live demonstrations, and recently returned to the Balearic Islands to help Karen set up her isolated Ibizan beach restaurant, 'Cala Bonita'.

This is Emma's first cookbook.

INDEX

Smith Street Books

Published in 2018 by Smith Street Books
Collingwood | Melbourne | Australia
smithstreetbooks.com

ISBN: 978-1-925418-84-2

Copyright text © Emma Warren
Copyright photography © Rochelle Eagle
Copyright illustrations © Daniel New
Copyright landscape photography © Shutterstock and Unsplash.com

CIP data is available from the National Library of Australia

Publisher: Lucy Heaver
Cover designer: Daniel New
Design concept: Daniel New
Design layout: Heather Menzies, Studio31 Graphics
Photographer: Rochelle Eagle
Food stylist: Lee Blaylock
Proofreader: Ariana Klepac
Indexer: Helena Holmgren
Home economists: Emma Warren, Rachael Lane, Gabrielle Evans

Printed & bound in China by C&C Offset Printing Co., Ltd.

Book 68
10 9 8 7 6 5 4 3 2 1